THE Cardmaker's BIBLE

160 INSPIRATIONAL CARD DESIGNS AND DEFINITIVE CARDMAKING TECHNIQUES

edited by cheryl brown

D&C

David and Charles

www.rucraft.co.uk

A DAVID & CHARLES BOOK

© F&W Media International, LTD 2011

David & Charles is an imprint of F&W Media
International, LTD
Brunel House, Forde Close, Newton Abbot, TQ12 4PU, UK

F&W Media International, LTD is a subsidiary of F+W
Media, Inc.

4700 East Galbraith Road, Cincinnati, OH 45236

First published in the UK and USA in 2011

Text and designs © Julie Hickey, Francoise Read,
Elizabeth Moad, Marion Elliot, Dorothy Wood,
Corinne Bradd, Joanne Sanderson, Sue Nicholson
and Shirley Toogood 2011

Layout and photography © F&W Media International,
LTD 2011

Julie Hickey, Francoise Read, Elizabeth Moad, Marion
Elliot, Dorothy Wood, Corinne Bradd, Joanne Sanderson,
Sue Nicholson and Shirley Toogood have asserted
their right to be identified as authors of this work in
accordance with the Copyright, Designs and Patents
Act, 1988.

A catalogue record for this book is available from the
British Library.

ISBN-13: 978-0-7153-3912-1 paperback
ISBN-10: 0-7153-3912-5 paperback

Printed in China by RR Donnelley
for F&W Media International LTD,
Brunel House, Forde Close, Newton Abbot, TQ12 4PU, UK

10 9 8 7 6 5 4 3 2 1

Publisher Alison Myer
Desk Editor Jeni Hennah
Project Editor Cheryl Brown
Art Editor Sarah Underhill
Photographers Karl Adamson, Kim Sayer, Ginette
Chapman and Simon Whitmore
Senior Production Controller Kelly Smith

F+W Media Inc. publishes high quality books on a
wide range of subjects. For more great book ideas visit:
www.rucraft.co.uk

CONTENTS

Introduction

The Cardmaker's Bible is designed to be your essential step-by-step guide to cardmaking occasions and techniques. In all 160 card designs are included, and, helpfully, these are organized into three card-giving sections.

A Cardmaker's Calendar Designs to celebrate the seasonal events throughout the year.

Life's Special Moments Features cards to commemorate memorable events and personal achievements.

Birthdays For each and every person's special day, with designs to suit all ages and interests.

No doubt, you are keen to make your choice of card and get started straight away, but it will pay in the long run if you take the time to get to grips with a few fundamentals, so take the time to review Cardmaker's Basics before you begin.

Card Dimensions

For the card measurements are in this book the height is given first and then the width, so a card of 20 x 10cm (8 x 4in) is 20cm (8in) high and 10cm (4in) wide.

The cards included use a wide range of papercraft techniques, from die-cutting to tea bag folding. Making a card is a great way to try your hand at a new technique, and, if this is the case, you will find the Techniques section at the back of the book invaluable, providing advice on tools and materials, outlining the rudimentary skills and exploring creative ideas.

CARDMAKER'S BASICS

In this section, you'll find a helpful guide to the tools that you will regularly need when making cards, essential advice on choosing and using glues, invaluable information on selecting and decorating card and paper, and a few simple skills that will ensure that your cardmaking is a success every time.

Essential Tools

The tools itemized below are likely to be needed for most card projects that you undertake, but if you are a regular crafter, the likelihood is that you will have many of these already. If you have a passion for a particular type of cardmaking technique – stamping, die-cutting or quilling for example – you will need more specialist tools, and details of these can be found in the Techniques section at the back of the book.

1 SCISSORS The essentials are a standard pair for trimming, a very small pair for cutting intricate shapes, and a non-stick pair for tacky items. Start a collection of fancy-edged scissors for jazzing up your cards

2 PENCILS Select an HB pencil for marking edges to be cut and a softer 2B pencil when lines will later be erased. A pencil will be needed for tracing off templates, for which you will also need tracing paper.

3 ERASER Use a hard Xyron adhesive eraser for removing excess adhesive and stubborn marks and a soft artist's putty rubber to remove pencil marks.

4 PENCIL SHARPENER Use a good-quality sharpener that doesn't chew up the wood. One with a case will help you to keep your workspace clean.

5 BONE FOLDER To help you achieve professional looking folds.

6 RULER For accurate measuring use a transparent plastic ruler, but when cutting with a craft knife, use a metal ruler

7 CRAFT KNIFE Use a craft knife with a sharp blade to produce a crisp cut, and always use with a self-healing cutting board.

8 SELF-HEALING CUTTING BOARD In addition to cutting, these mats are very useful as a firm base for stamping, although you should never use with a heat gun.

9 PAPER TRIMMER A cutter will make short work of cutting rectangles and squares.

10 PAINTBRUSHES Choose a selection including a fine brush for details.

11 SPONGE DAUBERS Designed to fit on your index finger, these are used to apply inks to backgrounds and stamped images. Although ordinary sponges can be used instead, the sponged effect is more even and your hands stay clean.

12 HOLE PUNCHES Available in a variety of sizes, the 1.5mm (1/16in), 3mm (1/8in) and 6mm (1/4in) are the most useful. Use to make holes for brads, eyelets, wire and ribbon. An 'anywhere' hole punch is useful for hard-to-reach places.

13 HEAT GUN Use to melt embossing powders, heat shrink plastic, and speed up the drying of paint/pens. Always work on a heat-resistant board.

14 EMBOSSING TOOL Use to score card, frost vellum and to emboss metal foil. These are available in fine, medium and large ball sizes. When using on vellum, work over a foam mat.

15 PAPER PIERCER Useful for making holes in card for sewing or for brads.

16 CORNER ROUNDER PUNCH Invaluable for rounding the corners of card, which is difficult to do accurately with scissors.

17 TWEEZERS Helpful for picking up and lifting delicate items such as gemstones and stickers.

18 ANTI-STATIC PUFF Use this to wipe card before stamping and embossing to reduce the static that holds stray specks of powder on the surface.

19 EYELET SETTER, HAMMER AND PUNCH Essential for setting eyelets and snaps, which are often used to attach panels to cards, for threading cord through, or as a purely decorative embellishment.

20 WATERCOLOUR PENCILS AND FELT-TIP PENS It is surprising how many times you will use these pencils and pens in your projects, so invest in a packet of each in a variety of colours.

safety tip

If your craft knife does not have a retractable blade, stick the blade into a cork to make it safe when not in use.

Glues

Different types of glue and adhesive are required in cardmaking for particular purposes, so it is important to keep a range in your kit to achieve the best results.

SUPERGLUE This is useful when you need a long-lasting adhesion and for gluing heavier-weight embellishments to cards, such as wiggly eyes and polymer clay.

safety tip Superglue is very powerful and must be used with extreme care. Keep it well out of reach of children. It will also mark work surfaces.

CLEAR ADHESIVE DOTS Available in different sizes and thicknesses, these easy-to-use dots come on a paper strip that is simply pressed face down onto the required area.

tip Use repositional adhesive dots to temporarily adhere items to try out an arrangement of elements on a card.

PVA (WHITE) GLUE This inexpensive water-based, all-purpose glue becomes transparent when dry, and is best used for delicate work, applied with the tip of a cocktail stick (toothpick).

GLUE STICKS These tubes of solid glue, which can be rubbed over large areas, are good for applying an even coat of adhesive that won't make the paper soggy.

GLUE PEN These are ideal for attaching small items as the pens have fine nibs. The glue comes out blue but dries clear.

GLITTER GLUES These are available in a wide range of colours and are intended for decorative purposes only (see Embellishments).

DOUBLE-SIDED TAPE This comes in a variety of widths although a narrow 5mm (¼in) is probably most useful. Pieces or lengths are cut and stuck down, and then the backing strip removed to reveal the second adhesive surface. It is ideal for mounting work behind an aperture. You can also punch shapes from it, then stick foil, glitter or beads to them.

ADHESIVE FOAM PADS Available in a block of small pads or individual larger pads, these are sticky on both sides and raise whatever is glued to them away from the surface for a 3D effect.

SILICONE GEL This clear gel, applied direct from the tube, both glues and adds depth. It dries clear and solid, making it suitable for 3D découpage and other crafting purposes where adhesive foam pads may not be suitable.

SPRAY ADHESIVE This glue in a spray can is very useful when a complete and even covering of adhesive is required, when sticking serviettes to card for example.

MASKING TAPE This is useful for keeping items temporarily in place.

safety tip Always use aerosol sprays in a well-ventilated room; spray onto the surface within a cardboard box.

Choosing Paper and Card

With such an abundance of card and paper to choose from, it can be a daunting task, especially if you are new to cardmaking. Illustrated here are just a few of the options on offer to you, but this really is just scratching the surface. To help you make good buying choices, listed below are various issues you will need to consider.

Texture

Paper and card comes in an array of textures from smooth to hammered. Other popular textures include linen- and watercolour-effect, ridged and embossed. Keep a supply of A4 (US letter) card in various colours and patterns – white and cream are your essentials but try to broaden your choices as much as possible scoring and folding your own cards (see Essential Skills).

Weight

Card and paper weight is measured in grammes per square metre (gsm). Choose a 260gsm card if you want your card to stand up without buckling, and a thinner card, for example 140gsm, for making cut-outs to stick to a base card or for making templates.

tip It may be difficult to find patterned card in the weight you require, but it is easy to cover your base card using the wide range of patterned papers available (see overleaf).

Finish

Some card and papers are not coated but left plain and matt, while others may have a glossy, metallic or pearlescent finish. An ornate card may only need a simple design to make it look truly stunning.

Types of paper

Some of the wide range of choices available include:

HANDMADE PAPER These tend to be porous and often contain dried leaves and petals. One of the most popular types is mulberry paper, which has lovely wispy edges when torn.

VELLUM This translucent non-porous paper looks a bit like tracing paper and is available in a variety of colours, patterns and finishes, including embossed. Specialist inks are required for stamping, and the surface of vellum can be dry embossed for a fantastic frosted effect. Vellum is best fixed with eyelets, and glue should be avoided as it can cause buckling.

WATERCOLOUR PAPER A heavyweight paper designed to be wetted without stretching and therefore suitable for painting on.

DECORATIVE CRAFT PAPER These include stardust papers, felt and flock paper, holographic, shimmer, metallic and pearlescent papers, and are available in different weights and thicknesses.

SCRAPBOOK PAPERS There is a huge choice of different designs, from floral and optical effects, to animal prints, camouflage and denim effect. Most come in collections of plain and coordinating patterned papers, which means you can mix and match colours and designs easily. They vary in thickness and some are available that are double-sided with different patterns or colours on the reverse, which is interesting for paper folding techniques such as iris folding.

tip Scrapbook papers can be used as a background; alternatively cut out individual motifs and use as an embellishment.

Ready–to–use cards

You can use pre-cut, pre-folded cards known as blanks which come in specific sizes with envelopes. They often have a window (known as an aperture) cut in them, through which you can display photos stickers and other embellishments. Although blanks work out more expensive than making your own base cards, they are handy if you are in a hurry. As well as rectangular-, square- and triangle-shaped pre-folded cards, many are available cut into particular shapes, such as handbags, shirts, shoes, fans and cards.

tip Most acetate is too thick to be folded into a professional-looking card so you will need to buy mechanically scored and folded clear card if it is required.

Decorating Card

Described below are some simple ways to decorate either ready-to-use card blanks or base cards that you have made yourself.

Cover a card with patterned paper

Use this method to produce a professional result when using a printed scrapbooking paper as a background for a card. There won't be any unsightly peeling at the edges because the paper extends around the fold to the back of the card.

Step One Cut the paper 1.3cm (½in) larger than the card on three sides, and long enough to cover the card front and a quarter of the back. Glue the card front and press down onto the back of the paper, leaving space all around to trim.

Step Two Lay the card front face down on a cutting mat and allow it to close. Trim away the excess paper from three sides of the card. Trim the overlap to about a quarter of the width of the card back if necessary.

Step Three Spread glue over the overlap area on the back of the card and press the paper down onto it. Close the card and re-crease the fold.

Make a multicoloured background

An amazing multicoloured background can be quickly created using a brayer (a paint roller used to ink up large stamps) and a rainbow inkpad.

Step One Anchor the pad down with your spare hand and ink up the brayer by rolling back and forth over the surface of the inkpad. Keep spinning it around when it is off the pad so that it is evenly covered. Roll it ever so slightly from side to side to lose the defined colour bands.

Step Two Working on a sheet of scrap paper, place the card to be decorated in the centre. Roll the brayer back and forth over the surface of the card, keeping to the same tracks. Press down hard and work quickly. Keep rolling until a good coverage is achieved (you may need to re-load the brayer).

Step Three If the card is wider than the brayer, repeat Step 2. Re-roll over the edge of the last colour band to create a small overlap.

tip For an interesting effect, wrap several elastic bands around the length of the brayer before inking.

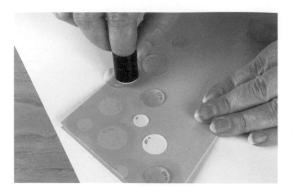

Make an embossed background

Embossing can give a plain single fold card extra interest. Work with embossing stencils over a light box, or for ease of use, invest in an embossing system, such as the Fiskars® ShapeBoss™, which does not require a light box. The background of Big Birthday Balloons was embossed using the 'Creative Sampler' embossing stencil set. The card is opened flat and inserted between the two layers of the stencil under a selected shape. You will be working in reverse, so it is only necessary to emboss the right-hand side of the card. Four shapes were chosen – a star, squiggle, line and swirl – from the many on the stencil. These were randomly embossed over the card, and the background was moved along, down or around to emboss them in a different place each time. A large ball embossing tool is used to apply a consistent downward pressure and outline the stencil design. Once the design is complete, remove the paper from the stencil, turn over and re-crease along the fold.

tip You can apply ink from a piece of sponge, sponge dauber or direct from an inkpad through stencils or around shapes for interesting effects. For soft backgrounds, lightly apply the ink, or for a stronger feature use more ink.

Sponge a background pattern

Combine sponging with masking to create an interesting all-over celebration bubbles pattern. The bubbles here have been die-cut from masking paper stuck to white card, so that they adhere to the surface while the ink is sponged around. The layer of masking paper is removed from the die-cut bubbles. Working from the top of the card down, place on the card and sponge pink ink over the edges of the masks. Lift the masks, place them further down and sponge again; repeat until the whole front is covered in bubbles.

Sponge a border strip

Tear a piece of scrap paper and place parallel to one edge of a sheet of coloured paper, in this case blue, leaving a border of blue paper. Dab the sponge of a light blue inkpad over the torn edge of the scrap paper onto the blue paper. Continue sponging all the way along the torn edge. Move the blue paper around to sponge the other edges in the same way, to create a soft border. Discard the scrap paper.

Essential Skills

Although you can buy pre-cut cards of many shapes and sizes, you may wish to make your own from a special piece of card, or you may have a card that you want to use but it does not have an aperture. These are just two of the simple techniques covered here to ensure that you always achieve professional-looking results. Other essential skills featured include positioning design elements, tearing and cutting paper, and making a simple pop-up insert.

Cutting and folding a single fold card

Following these three steps it is possible to make two cards roughly 15 x 10cm (6 x 4in)
– the card size most often used in this book – from just one sheet of A4 (US letter).

Step One Measure half the length of an A4 (US letter) card, and cut to size with a paper trimmer (or use a metal ruler and craft knife on a cutting mat). You now have two A5 cards.

Step Two Measure half the length of one of the A5 cards, and mark. Place in the paper trimmer lining the mark up with the groove that cuts the card. Starting at the top, pull an embossing tool down the groove to score the card.

Step Three Fold the card, aligning the edges and use a bone folder held flat to carefully flatten the crease.

tip Specialist boards are available with markings for making complex folds, such as gatefold and concertina cards, and card presentation boxes. Although not essential, they do produce great results in seconds.

Cutting apertures by hand

Mark and cut apertures on the card front. Cut out with a craft knife against a metal ruler placed on the good area so that if the knife slips it will cut into the area to be removed. When cutting the apertures, turn the card as you cut so that you always draw the knife towards you. Make sure that your cuts don't extend beyond the marked lines. When you have cut all four sides of the aperture, if the central portion fails to fall away, use the craft knife to cut the corners carefully so that it does so (do not pull out or you will damage the corners).

Cutting apertures with a punch

Although most often used to create paper shapes, craft punches can also create fancy apertures, as shown here.

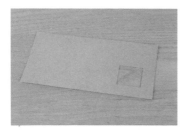

Step One Slide the card into the craft punch and press down to cut out the shape. When cutting out three apertures, line up the side of the punch with the top edge to make the first cut. Make the lowest aperture by lining up the punch with the bottom edge.

Step Two For the final aperture find the centre of the card and mark it. Find the centre of the punch and mark that too, then align the marks to cut out the aperture. Tidy up ragged edges of card by rubbing gently with an emery board or nail file.

Experiment with different arrangements of punched windows for eye-catching and unusual effects. It may help to punch the holes first and then cut the card to size.

Positioning design elements

It can be tricky to position a panel correctly onto a base card without a lopsided finish. This technique makes use of double-sided tape to allow you to move the element around and reposition it until you have it perfectly placed before sticking it down.

Step One Attach double-sided tape to the edges of the element to be stuck to the base card. Then pull back just enough backing paper so that you can see the paper tabs from the front of the card.

Step Two Position the element on your card, moving it around until you are completely happy with the position. Firm down where the tape is exposed.

Step Three Carefully hold the element in the centre and pull the paper tabs off completely. Firm down on the card.

tip Always change the blade of a craft knife regularly so that you avoid using a blunt blade that might tear the card.

Cutting and tearing paper

The cleanest cuts are made with a flat, clean surface, a sharp craft knife and metal ruler, and a steady hand. As an alternative to cutting, a torn edge adds an interesting dimension and can break up an otherwise uniform edge.

CUTTING WITH A CRAFT KNIFE
Keep the blade of the craft knife at a 45 degree angle when cutting. Draw the knife across the paper, but don't press too hard or the paper will wrinkle and an uneven edge will be left. When cutting thick paper, draw the blade across once without too much pressure, then again with more pressure to make the final cut.

TEARING WITH THE GRAIN
Tearing with the grain is easy and can produce a relatively straight line, as the paper naturally wants to tear this way. If you are not sure of the grain of a particular paper, test first by tearing a small piece of the paper.

TEARING WITH A RULER
If straight but torn lines are required, use a ruler as a guide. Hold the ruler firmly with one hand and pull the paper up and towards you with the other hand.

tip Be careful when tearing vellum, as it seems to tear easily in one direction and unpredictably.

Making a simple pop-up

A pop-up insert can bring a card design to life. Slits are made in a piece of thick printed paper that is then fixed inside a single fold card to make a 3D feature. The insert described is for a 15 x 10cm (6 x 4in) but can be adapted to measure any size card.

Step One Cut a piece of printed paper 15 x 20cm (6 x 8in) and fold in half. Measure 6cm (2³⁄₈in) up from the bottom and make a 6cm (2³⁄₈in) horizontal slit across the fold line.

Step Two Fold the paper and crease at the left and right side where the slit ends. This will make a tab that pops up once the card is open.

Step Three To make a second tab, cut slits 4.5cm (1¾in) and 5.5cm (2¹⁄₈in) down from the top of the patterned paper making the slits about 4.5cm (1¾in) wide. Glue to the base card but do not put glue on the pop-up parts, otherwise they will not pop up.

Embellishments

Embellishments add decorative detail and a personalized look to your card designs. The selection available in-store and online is amazing as can be seen below. Also very popular are peel-off stickers; for more on these turn to the Techniques section.

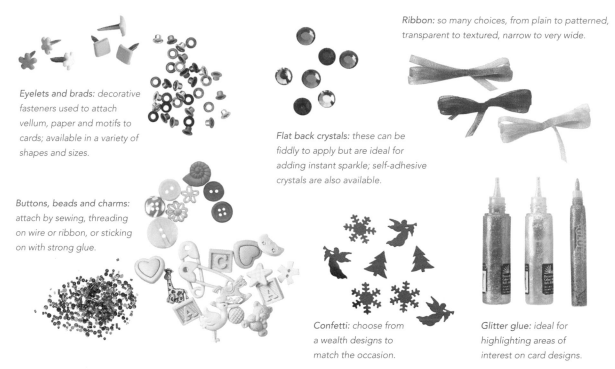

Eyelets and brads: decorative fasteners used to attach vellum, paper and motifs to cards; available in a variety of shapes and sizes.

Buttons, beads and charms: attach by sewing, threading on wire or ribbon, or sticking on with strong glue.

Ribbon: so many choices, from plain to patterned, transparent to textured, narrow to very wide.

Flat back crystals: these can be fiddly to apply but are ideal for adding instant sparkle; self-adhesive crystals are also available.

Confetti: choose from a wealth designs to match the occasion.

Glitter glue: ideal for highlighting areas of interest on card designs.

Fitting Eyelets

Eyelets are used on many of the cards included in this book to attach layered panels to the base card or for finishing off the threading hole of a tag embellishment. They are easy to fit and give a very professional finish

Step One Using an HB pencil, mark on the card the position of the eyelets. Working on an old cutting mat, place the eyelet hole punch over the pencil mark. Hammer down onto the tool to punch a hole.

Step Two Insert the eyelet into the punched hole. Working on the wrong side of the card, place the setting tool over the eyelet. Hit the top of the setting tool with the hammer to flatten the back of the eyelet.

Step Three The backs of the eyelets should be rounded and as smooth against the card as possible. Once eyelets are set, they cannot be removed.

Transferring Patterns

Depending on the card design you select, you may need to transfer a pattern from the Templates section at the back of the book.

Making a card template

Trace your chosen pattern. Place the tracing face down onto thin white card and draw over the lines to transfer the pattern. Cut out the template and draw around it onto the paper or card of your choice.

Direct transferral

To transfer the pattern directly onto your paper or card, place your tracing face down and carefully draw over the lines again with a pencil. Remove the tracing and lightly draw over the lines again if they are a little faint.

If a reverse shape is required, turn the template over and draw around it again before cutting the shapes out.

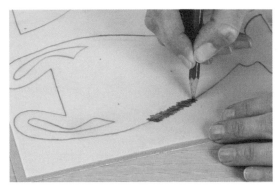

if you don't feel confident about following the line of the pattern neatly, place the tracing face down and scribble over the lines to transfer them. Then flip the tracing back the right way and redraw over the original lines to transfer the pattern.

tip If you cut out designs carefully with a craft knife, you can save both portions of the card so that you have a stencil and a template.

Using a scanner or photocopier

If you have a computer scanner you can scan your template into your computer and then print it out onto thin card. This enables you to store your template safely for further use and easily enlarge or reduce it to suit your requirements. Alternatively, you can photocopy it directly onto card.

The Cardmaker's Calendar

There are plenty of opportunities to make and give cards throughout the calendar year from Valentines Day to Christmas Day and this section is packed full of ideas for all of the most important ones.

A stamped 3D decoupage bunny for Easter and a pop-up posy for Mother's Day are just two of the fantastic springtime card designs featured, while for summer celebrations there is a wonderful iris folded party invitation and a gift-boxed shirt for Father's Day.

A brightly-embossed pumpkin card will brighten up those long autumn days, while a hand-stitched stocking and a novelty-shaped gingerbread man design are just two of the great choices for your Christmas greetings.

HEART STRINGS

Valentines Day (14th February) is a time for showing those we love how much we care. And what better expression of affection than a pair of hearts tied together with a beautiful silver string? This simple stamped motif is transformed into a unique image by adding hand-stitched detail.

you will need

♡ white linen-effect single fold card 16 x 11cm (6¼ x 4½in)

♡ white, black and silver linen-effect card

♡ thin white paper

♡ black, silver and grey printed paper

♡ pair of hearts rubber stamp

♡ graphite black Brilliance™ inkpad

♡ silver and black fine-tip, and pink and black gelly roll pens

♡ heart punch

♡ silver embroidery thread and sewing needle

Step One Stamp the image onto white card. Re-ink and stamp again onto semi-transparent white paper. Draw in the strings and evenly spaced (stitching) dots with the fine-tip pen. Place the paper over the card and align the hearts. Working on a foam mat, use a paper piercer to transfer the stitching holes onto the card.

Step Two Remove the paper and discard. Use the paper piercer to enlarge the stitching holes. Make sure the holes are large enough for the needle to pull through easily – if you have to tug too hard, you may crease the card.

Step Three Secure the silver thread to the card back with a small piece of adhesive tape before you start stitching to avoid an unsightly knot when you layer up the panel.

Step Four Sew backstitches through the pierced holes. Do not pull too hard when you begin stitching, otherwise you could release the thread. When you have completed the stitching, secure the other end of the thread with adhesive tape.

Step Five Colour in the silver areas on the hearts first, then the pink areas; allow to dry before using the black gelly roll pen. Trim the card to 11.5 x 7.5cm (4½ x 3in). Tie a length of silver thread in a bow, apply glue to the back of the knot and stick on where the balloon strings cross.

Step Six Punch out tiny hearts from silver and black card. Use a pencil dot to mark where you want the hearts to go and stick in place. Layer the stamped panel onto a panel of black then silver card. Glue a wide strip of the printed paper down the left-hand side of the single fold card and edge with a thin strip of black card. Attach the balloon panel with adhesive foam pads.

tip Try out the spacing of the holes on scrap card to see if it is workable – if they are too close together, the card could split when stitching.

Quick and Easy Valentines

Taking only minutes to make, the background for this simple yet romantic card is made from a rose design serviette.

you will need
- ♡ white single fold card 15cm (6in) square
- ♡ white card with gold shimmer
- ♡ paper serviette with rose design
- ♡ nine gold metal hearts
- ♡ narrow red sheer ribbon

tip Place the card in a box to spray; smooth the serviette onto the card using your fingers to smooth out the creases.

Separate the layers of the serviette; stick the patterned layer to the white single fold card using spray adhesive. Make a tag from the white card with gold shimmer. Decorate the tag with a torn piece of serviette and add three gold metal hearts and a ribbon bow. Three hearts top right and bottom left finish the card.

Kiss Me Quick

Use a funky lips rubber stamp and sizzling pink ink to create a passionate Valentines greeting.

you will need
- ♡ cream single fold card 15cm (6in) square
- ♡ white and fuchsia card
- ♡ lips rubber stamp
- ♡ pink inkpad
- ♡ flat back crystals

Randomly stamp lips all over the cream single fold card and one pair of lips in the middle of a 5cm (2in) white card square; then leave to dry. Mount the white card on top of a slightly larger fuchsia card square with double-sided tape. Stick the panel in the middle of the base card with adhesive foam pads. Add a crystal to each corner and three in the bottom right-hand corner.

With All My Love

Coloured ink and bold graphic stamps are used to make this quick and simple heart-themed card.

you will need
- ♡ mid-pink single fold card 14 x 10.5cm (5½ x 4⅛in)
- ♡ white and dark pink card
- ♡ pink printed paper
- ♡ hearts and block border rubber stamps
- ♡ pearlescent orchid Brilliance™ inkpad
- ♡ cranberry ColorBox® inkpad

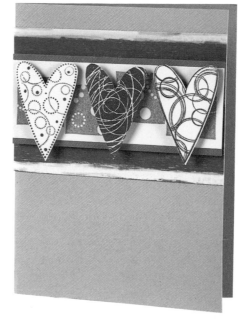

Use the cranberry inkpad to stamp the hearts on three small pieces of white card and cut out. Use the pearlescent orchid inkpad to stamp the block border onto a strip of white card, and layer onto a slightly larger strip of dark pink card to make the border panel. Glue a large strip of pink printed paper onto the top half of the single fold card. Use adhesive foam pads to stick the hearts onto the border panel; then stick centrally onto the patterned paper strip.

Two Hearts as One

A border punch has been used to give this Valentines a romantic lacy edging, and the punched hearts from the border decorate the card front.

you will need
- ♡ red single fold card 10 x 15cm (4 x 6in)
- ♡ mid-pink paper 20 x 15cm (8 x 6in)
- ♡ light pink paper 11.5 x 15cm (4½ x 6in)
- ♡ border punch
- ♡ two laser-cut gold hearts

Score and fold the mid-pink paper in half and punch a border along one edge, saving the punched-out hearts. Stick the paper over the red single fold card. Punch along one edge of the light pink paper; score and fold along 2.5cm (1in) from the opposite edge of the paper and stick on top of the mid-pink paper so that the punched borders lay one above the other. Stick on the laser-cut gold hearts centrally and randomly scatter punched hearts over the card front.

EASTER BUNNY

The giving and receiving of brightly decorated eggs is an Easter tradition. This cute image shows the Easter bunny delivering his chocolate treats. Printing and layering selected motifs from a set of clear stamps creates a 3D effect. For more on using clear stamps, see Techniques: Stamping.

you will need

- white textured single fold card 16 x 11cm (6¼ x 4½in)
- smooth white card
- yellow and green printed papers
- large and tiny Easter bunny, basket, egg border and small flower set of clear stamps
- clear acrylic block
- graphite black Brilliance™ inkpad
- brush marker colour pens
- fine-tip black pen
- green brad

Step One Stamp three large bunnies, one basket, one egg border and one tiny bunny onto smooth white card. Run the brush marker pens over a plastic lid. Dip a fine paintbrush into clean water, pick up some of the ink and colour in the images. To add depth, paint a pale blue line around the edge of the bunny pieces.

Step Two Use a small, sharp pair of scissors to cut out the images, cutting very slightly into the outline so that none of the white card remains. Use a craft knife on a cutting mat to cut away the inside section of the basket.

Step Three Keeping one large bunny intact, remove the back leg and paw from another bunny and all but the head and arm from the remaining one. Cut out the eggs you need from the egg border.

Step Four Place adhesive foam pads on the back of the sections for layering, spacing them out so that there is support all round the edges and in the centre. Add the layers to the whole bunny.

tip Write a surprise message on the card front, which is revealed only when the tag is swung to one side.

Step Five Cut a large tag from the yellow paper and stamp a small flower motif at random all over. Colour in the flowers. Glue a strip of green paper to the bottom of the yellow tag. Draw on small dotted lines (for clumps of grass). Cut a thin green paper strip, fold in half at an angle and glue onto the tag.

Step Six Mount the bunny onto the tag. Attach the two eggs to the basket back; slide the basket between the bunny's paws and over the back foot. Use tweezers to tuck the single egg in between the bunny's paws. Mount the tiny bunny with adhesive foam pads. Glue a band of yellow paper to the card front and attach the tag with the brad. Stamp flowers along the bottom of the card and colour in.

A Cracking Easter Card

A single oval punch is perfect for creating an egg shape, and the embellishments in tangy citrus colours give a fresh, spring look.

you will need

- cream single fold card 14.8 x 10.5cm (5¾ x 4⅛in)
- yellow card
- oval punch
- yellow striped and daisy embossed paper
- medium, small and tiny orange buttons
- yellow embroidery thread
- narrow orange daisy printed ribbon

Cut a panel of yellow striped paper slightly smaller than the single fold card and attach with double-sided tape. Tie a couple of strands of embroidery thread through four medium-sized buttons and glue one in each corner. Stick a strip of daisy embossed paper across the centre of the card with double-sided tape. Punch a yellow card oval; decorate with tiny and small threaded buttons and add a ribbon bow. Secure the decorated 'egg' using adhesive foam pads.

More Easter Bunnies

The stamp used for this design is very versatile as the whole image can be used or just the little rabbits separately.

you will need

- cream card 10.5 x 14.8cm (4⅛in x 5¾in)
- green and pastel printed papers
- bunny pots rubber stamp
- colouring pencils
- small egg punch

Stamp the image across the middle of the cream card, cut away (see Teddy Twins, Steps 1–3) and colour in. Punch eggs from the pastel papers. Hand tear a piece of green printed paper and glue to the bottom edge; decorate with additional stamped bunnies and eggs.

St Patrick's Day

Those with Irish roots enjoy a good party on 17th March, and this clover card will wish them all the best.

you will need

- cream single fold card 17.5 x 8cm (7 x 3¹⁄₈in) with three square apertures
- green flock paper
- heart punch
- green flat back crystals

Punch nine hearts from the green flock paper. Working from the front of the card, arrange the hearts in cloverleaf shapes inside each aperture. Cut thin stems from the flock paper and use a glue pen to stick all the pieces down. Highlight the corner of each square with a flat back crystal.

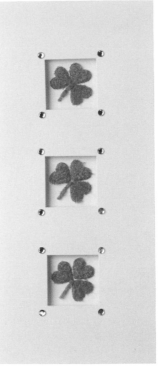

St David's Day

This card is ideal for Welsh friends celebrating on 1st March, but it's cheerful quilled daffodil decoration makes it perfect for any springtime celebration.

you will need

- light green single fold card 14.8 x 10.5cm (5¾ x 4¹⁄₈in)
- green paper
- yellow, orange and green 1cm (³⁄₈in) wide quilling paper strips
- yellow 3mm (¹⁄₈in) wide quilling paper strips
- quilling tool
- fancy-edged scissors

Glue a green paper panel onto the single fold card. For the petals, make five loose closed coils from 30cm (12in) lengths of the 3mm (¹⁄₈in) wide paper strips and pinch into teardrop shapes. Arrange in a circle at the top of the card, pulling the points of the inner parts in line with the pinched point as you glue them in place and leaving room in the centre for the trumpet. Make the daffodil trumpet (see Techniques: Quilling) and glue in place. For the stem, glue two lengths of 1cm (³⁄₈in) wide green paper together lengthways; cut a long narrow leaf with a pointed end.

tip For springtime greetings, make a narcissus by gluing white petals around the trumpet.

POP-OUT POSY

Although the timing may differ depending on the country, Mother's Day is celebrated all over the world. Make a real impact with a decorative ribbon-tied card that opens to reveal a surprise bouquet of flowers. The impact of the pop-up is enhanced by using bold printed card for the flowers, to contrast with the paler colour of the background.

you will need

- ❦ pink ribbed single fold card 16 x 10.5cm (6¼ x 4⅛in)

- ❦ mid-pink card 14.5 x 20cm (5¾ x 8in)

- ❦ spotted printed card, various designs

- ❦ burgundy, green, pink and orange card

- ❦ white paper

- ❦ pink, wine and olive green inkpads

- ❦ 1cm (½in) circle punch

- ❦ pink craft wire

- ❦ wire cutters

- ❦ round-nosed pliers

- ❦ narrow green ribbon

Step One Cut a piece of white paper 14.5 x 20cm (5¾ x 8in). Fold in half, open out and then directly trace the pop-up insert (see Templates) onto the paper so the centre fold lines match up. Lay this pattern on top of the mid-pink card and use a pin to mark the dots onto the card. Cut along the zigzag horizontal lines as shown.

Step Two Score the vertical lines between the top and bottom pinholes. Score the centre fold line of the card only as far down as the cut zigzag. Fold the card to carefully push out the pop-out. Firmly crease along all the lines (check the card folds flat). Cut the pop-out section from white paper and stick in place on the pink card.

Step Three Cut three flower heads and five leaf shapes and colour the edges by dabbing with the inkpads. Stick punched card circles in the flower centres. Score the leaves down the centre and stick three to the back of the card. Cut three thin green card stems and glue the flowers on; fix in place behind the pop-out section with the remaining leaves.

Step Four Cut two wide strips of spotted card. Stick one close to the right-hand edge of the card and one down the centre of the left-hand side. Make a small tag from green card and decorate with a strip of spotted card. Thread pink craft wire through the hole; twist together and coil each end. Stick ribbon across the pop-out section and trim neatly. Attach the tag.

Step Five Stick double-sided tape around the edge of the pop-up card panel on the reverse side. Stick a couple of pieces near the centre fold. Peel off part of the backing paper from the outer tape and all of it from the pieces on the fold. Position the card inside the base card, peel off the remaining backing paper and press in place.

Step Six Stick a 50cm (20in) length of ribbon across the back of the card just above the centre. Tie in a bow on the front of the card. Make a large tag from green card decorated with a spotted card strip. Punch a small hole at the top and thread ribbon through; tie in a knot and trim the ends at an angle. Tuck the tag under the ribbon bow to finish.

Blue Blooms

Flowers are a popular choice for Mother's Day and this beautiful stamped card with its unusual blended background will coordinate beautifully.

you will need

- light green linen-effect single fold card 16 x 11cm (6¼ x 4½in)
- white, blue and light green linen-effect card
- floral rubber stamp
- peacock Brilliance™ inkpad
- brilliant blue Mica Magic™ inkpad
- holographic glitter glue
- very narrow blue ribbon

tip The tag will stand out even more if you colour up the edges by pressing into an inkpad.

Dab a loose ball of clingfilm across the two greens on the Brilliance™ inkpad and use to decorate a white card panel, pressing gently. Using the Mica Magic™ inkpad, stamp the image onto the sponged card. Mount the panel on a piece of blue card cut slightly larger. Use the blue Brilliance™ inkpad to stamp the design across the base card. Make and stamp a light green tag; thread with ribbon. Mount the panel on; add the tag with adhesive foam pads. Add glitter glue highlights.

Bright Bouquet

This variation on the Pop-Out Posy is much simpler and faster to make as it uses a blank triangle card and a floral rubber stamp for the bouquet.

Heat emboss the image onto two pieces of white card each 10cm (4in) square. Colour in one image with brush marker pens. On the second, colour in two flower heads only; cut out and layer onto the whole image using adhesive foam pads. Cut a 9cm (3½in) square from patterned paper; fold the left and bottom side inwards so that they overlap to make a rough triangle shape and fix. Glue the stamped bouquet inside. Cover the base card with patterned paper. Secure the eyelets on the front and back so they lie next to each other when the card is closed. Tie the ribbon through and finish with a bow.

you will need

- white single fold triangle card
- white card
- patterned papers
- floral rubber stamp
- VersaMark™ inkpad
- gold embossing powder
- two gold eyelets
- narrow green ribbon

Sweet Treat

Mums will love this sweet little cupcake decorated with simple open coils and topped with a quilled carrot.

you will need

- orange single fold card 10 x 9cm (4 x 3½in)
- light green and orange card
- pink vellum
- light and dark pink 2mm (1/16in) wide quilling paper strips
- orange 3mm (1/8in) wide quilling paper strips
- green 1cm (3/8in) wide quilling paper strips
- quilling tool and 45 degree-angled fringing tool
- two pink brads

Cut the cupcake case from a scrap of orange card (see Templates) and stick to a light green card panel. Use an orange felt tip pen to draw lines on the cupcake case and to draw a dashed border around the edge of the green card. Top the cupcake with open coils made from 2mm (1/16in) paper strips and top with a single carrot (see Techniques: Quilling). Glue the green panel to the front of the single fold card, and use the pink brads to secure a hand-torn strip of vellum to the left-hand edge.

....

Time for Tea

The doors of this cupboard card open to reveal a collection of pretty teacups.

you will need

- white single fold card 10.5 x 14.5cm (4 1/8 x 5¾in)
- white card
- swirly pattern and teacups rubber stamps
- VersaMark™ inkpad
- lavender, sea glass and aqua ColorBox® inkpads
- clear embossing powder
- two large blue brads

Cut a piece of white card 10 x 14cm (4 x 5½in). Using the VersaMark™ inkpad, stamp the swirly pattern image on the left-hand side and heat emboss. Once dry, repeat on the right-hand side. Use the coloured inkpads to apply the ink in a swirling motion; wipe off the excess to reveal the embossed image. With a sharp craft knife cut along the top, bottom and centre of the stamped panel; score down the left and right edges and fold back the 'doors'. Add brad 'handles'. Stick the doors onto the base card. Stamp the teacups onto white card and cut out. To make the cupboard shelf, cut a thin strip of white card; colour and glue in place. Glue the teacups onto the shelves.

ONE IN A MILLION

Every father deserves a unique card to celebrate his special day and this Celtic design is ideal. The metal design is made from pure copper and amazing things happen when it is heated. It changes in colour from bright copper to tarnished orange, to pink then purple, and finally to a bluey silver and gold.

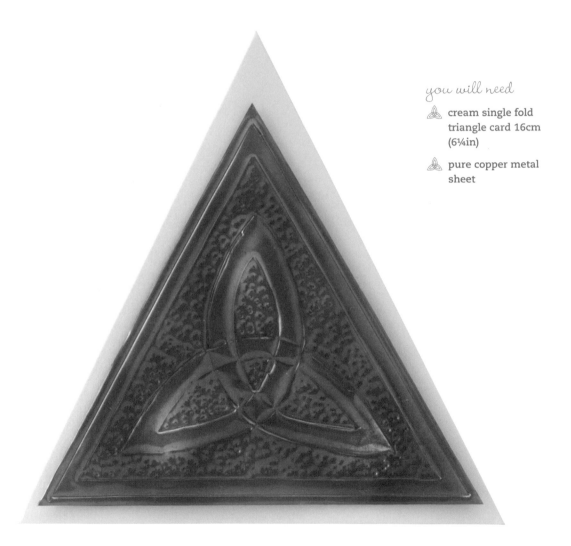

you will need

- **cream single fold triangle card 16cm (6¼in)**
- **pure copper metal sheet**

 tip   For more on working with metal, see Techniques: Metal and Wire.

Step One Make a tracing of the Celtic design (see Templates). Lay the copper sheet on top of a foam mat, place the design on top and carefully trace over the pencil lines with an embossing tool. You need to apply about the same pressure as you would for writing. As you work, lift up the tracing paper occasionally to see if the pattern is clear.

Step Two Working on a heat-resistant board, heat the copper sheet with the heat gun. The copper will change colour from bright copper to a tarnished orange. The copper changes colour exactly at the spot where the heat is directed.

Step Three Keep heating the copper sheet and it will change to a pinky colour, then to purple. Finally it will change to a bluey silver and gold. Leave until it has cooled completely.

Step Four Place the copper sheet on a foam mat and use a ruler and the embossing tool to draw a triangle around the design about 1.3cm (½in) away from it. Then draw a second triangle about 6mm (¼in) outside the first triangle.

Step Five Use the embossing tool with a stabbing motion to create a hammered effect on the metal. Don't go too close to the design or you will flatten out the edges and lose the pattern.

Step Six Use a guillotine (or a pair of scissors) to cut out the design, cutting just outside the second triangle outline. Stick to the front of the card using adhesive foam pads.

tip Do not touch the copper whilst heating it or directly afterwards, as it gets very hot and retains the heat for some time.

Father's Day Gift

This card features a rubber stamped man's shirt and tie. Real buttons add the perfect finishing touch.

you will need

- white card, two pieces 11 x 8cm (4³⁄₈ x 3¹⁄₈in)
- blue card, two pieces 11 x 8cm (4³⁄₈ x 3¹⁄₈in)
- white spotted paper 11 x 8cm (4³⁄₈ x 3¹⁄₈in)
- brown patterned paper 11 x 16cm (4³⁄₈ x 6¼in)
- shirt rubber stamp
- VersaMark™ inkpad
- black embossing powder
- four small white buttons

Stamp and heat emboss the image onto two pieces of blue card, one piece of white card and the white spotted paper (see Techniques: Heat Embossing). Cut the collar and cuffs from the white card, the pocket from one piece of the blue card and the tie from the white spotted paper. Use adhesive foam pads to stick the layers together over the whole shirt image, cut out from the second piece of blue card. Glue the buttons on. Fold the brown patterned paper in half to make a mini base card and stick the finished shirt on top.

DIY Dad

DIY Dads will love this unusual card and yet it is so simple to make with just a few special purchases.

Cut a 15 x 6cm (6 x 2⅜in) strip of floorboard printed paper and secure to the single fold card with double-sided tape. Add a screw head snap to each corner of the floorboard panel and three in the bottom right-hand corner of the card. Make a tag from cream card and decorate with a strip of floorboard printed paper. Stick the hammer to a small piece of cream card and attach to the tag with adhesive foam pads. Add string to the tag and fix to the card.

you will need

- bronze single fold card 15cm (6in) square
- cream card
- floorboard printed paper
- screw head snaps
- DIY hammer tool motif
- string

Gardening Dad

A pair of quilled shears is the main decoration here, but if time is short replace with a gardening sticker.

you will need

- green single fold card 15 x 10cm (6 x 4in)
- silver card
- green striped paper
- brown 3mm (⅛in) wide quilling paper strips
- quilling tool
- acetate
- raffia

Cut a 7cm (2¾in) square aperture in the front of the single fold card. Cut a piece of green striped paper slightly smaller than the card front; lay it over the card front to trace off the aperture and cut out. Glue the green striped paper panel to the front of the card with a sheet of acetate in between. Make two quilled cones for the shears' handles (see Techniques: Quilling), and cut the blade from the silver card (see Templates). Assemble the shears onto the acetate and tie raffia around the card spine to finish.

Take a Picture

This Father's Day card is personalized by putting photographs of the children in the patterned slide frame dome stickers.

you will need

- light blue single fold card 17.5 x 8cm (7 x 3¼in)
- black card
- parchment paper
- piece of scrap 35mm film negative
- silver camera peel-off sticker
- two patterned slide frame dome stickers
- two photographs

Cut a 5cm (2in) aperture in the centre of the single fold card. Cut and place two lengths of the film negative in opposite corners as a basic frame for the design. Stick a piece of parchment paper behind the aperture. Place the camera peel-off sticker onto black card, cut out and then glue to the parchment paper. Place the two patterned slide frame dome stickers over your chosen photographs and trim to size; glue on top of the film negative strips to hold them in place.

SUMMER SUN

What better way to celebrate the Summer Solstice (21st June) than holding a barbecue for family and friends? This dynamic sun design, created using the iris folding technique, is the perfect invitation for your longest day party. For more details on this compulsive paper folding method, see Techniques: Iris Folding.

you will need

- ✺ red two-fold card 12.5cm (4⅞in) square with round aperture 9cm (3½in) in diameter
- ✺ 30 strips of paper 10 x 2cm (4 x ¾in)
- ✺ holographic card
- ✺ yellow card

tip For the brightest effect choose three shades of orange and three shades of yellow, five strips of each.

Step One Fold all the strips in half lengthways and group according to their six colours. Photocopy the sun template (see Templates) and cut out. Place the template on your work surface, then place the two-fold card, opened out and right-side down, over the template so that you can see the template through the circular aperture of the card.

Step Two Place one strip of yellow paper, folded edge inwards, over line 1. Trim the ends and tape in place. Continue positioning the paper strips using a different colour each time and following the numbered sequence as marked on the template.

Step Three Keep working round the circle with the strips of paper, applying the strips in the same colour order with the folded edge inwards and following the numbered sequence. It will start to look untidy but don't worry as this side will not be seen.

Step Four As you get closer to the centre, the strips will get smaller, so you will need to trim off more.

Step Five When the last strip has been used, tape a 7 x 9cm (2¾ x 3½in) piece of holographic card, glossy-side down, over the remaining hole in the centre. Attach double-sided tape to all four edges of the central panel of the card on the inside. Remove the tape backing, fold the third section of the card over and press down firmly to make a single fold card.

Step Six Cut 12 triangles from the yellow card 2cm (¾in) high x 2cm (¾in) wide. Glue these to the front of the card around the aperture.

tip Use low-tack adhesive tape to hold the card over the template to keep it firmly in place.

37

Surfer's Paradise

This Hawaiian theme card celebrates all that is best about the summer – sun, sand and surf. The sunset colour was achieved by brayering.

Use the VersaMark™ inkpad to stamp the postage stamp block onto glossy card. Use the multicoloured Kaleidacolor™ inkpad and the brayer to create a sunset background. Trim to 10 x 12.5cm (4 x 4⅞in) and stamp with the surfboards design using the graphite black inkpad. Mount onto a black card panel and the orange single fold card in turn using the brads to secure. Decorate with stamped embellishments, punched flowers and shell beads.

you will need

- orange single fold card 12.5 x 15cm (5 x 6in)
- white glossy card A4 (US letter) sheet
- black card
- postage stamp block, Hawaiian shirt, surfboards and flip-flops rubber stamps

- VersaMark™ inkpad
- desert heat Kaleidacolor™ inkpad
- graphite black Brilliance™ inkpad
- brayer
- four black brads
- flower punch
- plastic shell beads

Beach Babe

A quilled polka-dot bikini on a sky-blue tag on a sunny yellow card is a hopeful sign of a long, hot summer ahead.

you will need

- yellow single fold card 15 x 10cm (6 x 4in)
- blue card tag
- gingham paper

- white and red 3mm (⅛in) wide quilling paper strips
- quilling tool and needle tool
- two miniature white ribbon bows

For the bikini top, make two loose closed coils with 40cm (15¾in) lengths of red paper; pinch into triangles. Make the bikini bottom from an 80cm (32in) length. Make a tight coil from a 5cm (2in) length of white paper; glue the two smaller triangles to either side and add a halter neck strap and ties. Make tiny tight closed white paper coils; insert into the bikini top and bottom. Glue gingham paper strips to the base card and the tag. Arrange the bikini on the tag and glue in place.

tip Instead of tiny coils, add glitter glue dots.

Summer Cocktail Party

A great invitation to a summer barbecue – rows of cocktails have highlights of glitter glue added for a touch of fizz.

you will need
- black single fold card 17 x 10.5cm (6¾ x 4¼in)
- magenta card
- multi-coloured spotted paper
- cocktails rubber stamp
- jet black StazOn™ inkpad
- yellow, orange and magenta permanent markers
- acetate
- five gold eyelets
- holographic glitter

Cut a piece of acetate 17 x 8cm (6¾ x 3¼in) and stamp on three evenly spaced rows of cocktails. When completely dry, colour in on the reverse with permanent markers. Cut a piece of magenta card slightly narrower than the black single fold card, and a piece of spotted paper slightly narrower again. Layer onto the base card. Secure the acetate panel to the base card with the eyelets, spacing them out between the rows of glasses. Add PVA (white) glue to the liquid in the glasses and sprinkle with the glitter.

tip Use a cutting mat with a printed grid when stamping on the acetate.

Independence Day

The Fourth of July is a very important day for Americans the world over and this simple card is full of patriotic pride.

you will need
- red single fold card 15cm (6in) square
- white sparkle, blue pearlescent and red card
- star punch

Tear five thin strips of white sparkle card and space evenly down the red single fold card. Secure with double-sided tape. Trace off the heart template (see Templates), transfer to the back of the blue card and tear out the shape. Punch out red stars and stick to the blue heart using a glue pen. Mount the heart onto the card using double-sided tape.

HARVEST FESTIVAL

Many countries celebrate the safe gathering in of the harvest as the nights grow longer and the leaves begin to fall. The range of autumnal shades in this card, including the copper wire and orange ribbon, work particularly well with the strong black embossed outlines of the stamped motifs. For more on heat embossing, see Techniques: Heat Embossing.

you will need

- mango single fold card 12cm (4¾in) square
- honey yellow and black card
- leaf and pumpkin rubber stamps
- black, marigold and orange pigment inkpads
- black and clear embossing powders
- two shades of green, orange and brown dual embossing pens
- 22-gauge copper wire and wire cutters
- black eyelet peel-off sticker
- orange sheer ribbon

Step One Cut a 10cm (4in) square of honey yellow card and place on some scrap paper. Using the black inkpad, randomly stamp leaves all over the card and its edges. Sprinkle black embossing powder all over, shake off the excess and heat with a heat gun to emboss.

Step Two Using the embossing pens, colour in the leaves – one leaf of the pair in the two shades of green and the other in orange and brown, four to five at a time – and cover with the clear embossing powder. Heat the embossing powder until it has melted. Allow to cool before continuing. Repeat until complete.

Step Three Starting with the lightest orange inkpad, sponge the ink over the panel in the gaps between the leaves. Add the darker orange in the same way, but this time apply less of it to allow the previous layer to show through. Using spray glue, mount the panel onto black card cut slightly larger, then mount at an angle on the single fold card.

Step Four Make a tag from honey yellow card. Using the black inkpad and black embossing powder, stamp and heat emboss the pumpkin on the tag.

Step Five Colour in the pumpkin, leaving some areas uncovered. Use mostly orange with touches of brown to add shading on the outer edges. Using a 1.5mm (1/16in) hole punch, make a hole either side of the pumpkin stalk.

Step Six Cut a short length of copper wire and bend it into a hairpin. Thread the ends through the tag holes from the back to the front and curl into loose coils. Fold and push the coils over each other and up against the surface of the tag. Decorate to finish: stick the peel-off over the hole and thread through the ribbon. Mount the tag centrally on the card with adhesive foam pads.

tip Sponge marigold and orange ink over the edges of the tag.

Falling Leaves

Warm colours are combined with copper, fabric and mesh for a lovely autumn celebration card.

you will need

- plum single fold card 15 x 10cm (6 x 4in)
- pure copper metal sheet
- metallic fabric strip and wire mesh scraps
- leaf punch

Draw a tag shape onto the copper sheet. Working on a heat-resistant board, heat the copper sheet with a heat gun until it changes colour. Leave to cool. Use an embossing tool to mark patterns on the tag. Cut out the tag and punch out two leaf shapes from it and discard. Punch three leaf shapes from the copper sheet. On the left-hand side of the card, layer the mesh and fabric and glue the three copper leaves evenly on top. Secure the copper tag to the top right-hand side to finish.

Hues of the Forest

Replicate the many colours of autumn leaves by multiple heat embossing (see Techniques: Heat Embossing for more details).

you will need

- green pearlescent single fold card 15 x 10cm (6 x 4in)
- copper and green pearlescent card
- large leaf rubber stamp
- VersaMark™ inkpad
- green inkpad
- four autumnal coloured embossing powders
- three copper snaps and tiny Diamond Dots™

tip Tiny Diamond Dots™ are have been used to highlight the central leaf.

Stamp leaves over green pearlescent card using the VersaMark™ inkpad. Randomly sprinkle the four embossing powders, one at a time, over the stamped leaves. Once dry lightly sponge between the leaves with green ink. Trim and layer on top of a copper card panel cut slightly larger. From the decorated card that remains, cut a small square and layer onto a square of copper card; mount with adhesive foam pads. Add copper snaps for a decorative border.

Invitation to Thanksgiving

Americans celebrate Thanksgiving on the fourth Thursday in November and get together for a traditional feast.

you will need

- light green single fold card 10 x 15cm (4 x 6in)
- white, red, gold, brown and green paper
- brown inkpad
- clingfilm
- red 3mm (¹/8in) wide quilling paper strips
- quilling tool

Use the glass, bottle, turkey and plate templates (see Templates) to make the decorations from coloured papers. Colour the turkey using a ball of scrunched up clingfilm pressed into the brown inkpad and dab over the front of the body and the leg. Make tight red quilled coils from 20cm (8in) lengths of the quilling paper strips and cut out green leaves freehand to adorn the turkey plate.

Golden Leaf Gatefold

This wonderful gatefold card celebrates autumn, 'the season of mists and mellow fruitfulness', and provides a more formal Thanksgiving invite.

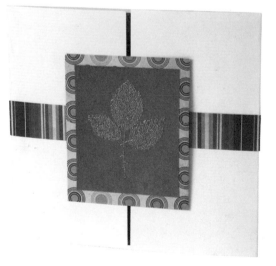

you will need

- white gatefold card 13cm (5¹/8in) square
- red card and green paper
- circle, striped, leaf and fruit printed papers
- leaf rubber stamp
- VersaMark™ inkpad
- gold embossing powder
- four green brads

Cut a narrow strip of striped paper and glue around the middle of the gatefold card. Cover one side of a rectangular piece of red card with circle paper and glue a panel of green paper cut slightly smaller on top. Stamp the leaf in the centre and heat emboss with the gold embossing powder. Glue to the left-hand panel on the front of the gatefold card. Cover the back of the inside of the card with fruit printed paper.

GHOSTLY GREETINGS

Who can resist the spooky thrills of Halloween (31st October)? Join in the fun and send a ghoulish greeting to family and friends. Here, the masking technique has been used to make one ghostly motif appear behind the other from a single stamp.

you will need

- orange single fold card 15cm (6in) square
- black glossy and white card
- JudiKins Masking Paper™
- ghouls rubber stamp
- cherry pink StazOn™ inkpad
- graphite black Brilliance™ inkpad
- lime pearlescent paint
- white and grey Liquid Appliqué™
- Plaid Clear Dimensional Magic™
- die-cutting tool and spider and bat dies
- wiggly eyes

Step One
Carefully unroll the masking paper and cut off a section large enough for the mask. Using the pink inkpad, ink the stamp up carefully. Check that the image is fully inked up, then stamp onto the masking paper. Leave the ink to dry while you clean the rubber stamp.

Step Two
Using small scissors, cut around the image, cutting into the stamped line to avoid the halo effect that can occur when stamping over an edge. Using the black inkpad, stamp onto a 13.5cm (5¼in) square of white card to the left of centre. Leave to dry, then place the mask over the image.

Step Three
Re-ink the stamp and make a second print of the motif, stamping the second ghoul partly over the mask. When the mask is removed, the first ghoul will be in the foreground and the second ghoul will appear to be peering cheekily over his shoulder.

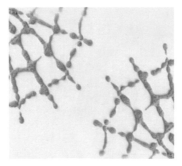

Step Four
Apply lime green pearlescent paint around the ghouls and paint the eyes and mouths. Leave to dry. Squeeze white Liquid Appliqué™ in random patches over both ghouls. Using a heat gun, apply heat to the Liquid Appliqué™, which will then rise and puff up.

Step Five
Use the grey Liquid Appliqué™ to draw a web in the panel corners. Leave to dry so that a hard shell forms. Paint over the eyes and teeth of both ghouls with the Dimensional Magic™.

Step Six
Die-cut the spider and two bats from black glossy card. Attach wiggly eyes to the spider with strong glue; mount onto the main panel with adhesive foam pads. To finish, mount the main panel on a 14cm (5½in) square of black glossy card, then onto the orange single fold card.

tip Rather than waiting for the Liquid Appliqué™ to dry, you can heat it straight after application while it is still wet, but the results are less predictable.

House Ghost

This card is constructed so that the ghost can be pulled up and down.

you will need

- white single fold card 18 x 13cm (7 x 5in)
- thin white card
- orange and charcoal grey scrapbooking papers
- light and dark orange, lime green and purple paper

Cover the single fold card with a grainy orange background paper for an ethereal glow. Cut the house from the grey scrapbooking paper and cut irregular-shaped windows from orange paper and a lime green door (see Templates). Cut a wide slit along the roofline before sticking the house to the card. Cut the ghost from thin white card; pop in the slit. Use a black felt-tip pen to add the windowpanes and the ghost's mouth and eyes. To finish add an angled purple paper strip at the base, and a crescent moon cut from dark orange paper.

Witch's Hat

Transform a simple triangular-shaped card into a witch's hat stamped with a bat motif and embossed with holographic powder.

you will need

- black single fold triangle card 20 x 20 x 15cm (8 x 8 x 6in)
- black, green, purple and orange card
- bat, cat, haunted house and pumpkin rubber stamps
- VersaMark™ inkpad
- black Brilliance™ inkpad
- holographic embossing powder
- die-cutting tool and frame die
- tag punch
- three black eyelets
- narrow orange gingham and sheer black ribbon

Using the VersaMark™ inkpad, stamp bats all over the triangle card and heat emboss. Cut the green card to fit at the base of the triangle and mount a black card strip along the bottom. Die-cut a purple card frame; tie on gingham ribbon and mount with adhesive foam pads. Using the black inkpad, stamp a cat, house and four pumpkins onto orange card. Punch out a cat and house tag. Cut out the pumpkins. Add black ribbon to the tags. Punch three holes in the hatband, set the eyelets and tie with ribbon. Mount the tags and pumpkins.

Halloween Magic

A spooky sticker or two and a touch of glitter glue
for a quick Halloween greetings card.

you will need

- cream single fold card 15cm (6in) square
- purple, green and orange card
- witch, spider and web stickers
- glitter glue
- orange gingham ribbon

Cut two pieces of purple card 11.5 x 6.5cm (4½ x 2⅝in) and
6 x 3cm (2⅜ x 1¼in); two pieces of green card 15 x 7 cm
(6 x 2¾in) and 6 x 2.5cm (2⅜ x 1in); and two pieces of orange card 15 x 8 cm (6 x 3⅛in) and 6 x 2cm
(2⅜ x ¾in). Stick the witch on the purple panel and mount onto the green panel. Tie the ribbon
around the base; mount onto the orange panel. Layer up the purple, green and orange strips;
decorate with spiders. Stick the witch panel and spider strip onto the base card. Stick the web sticker
to the corner; add glitter glue highlights.

Spooked Cat

A quilled black cat spotlighted in a vibrant orange circle
makes the perfect decoration for a Halloween party invitation.

you will need

- red single fold card 15 x 10cm (6 x 4in) with circle aperture
- orange paper
- black 3mm (⅛in) quilling paper strips
- black, yellow and pink 2mm (1/16in) wide quilling paper strips
- quilling tool
- narrow orange ribbon

For the cat's body, glue three 40cm (15¾in) lengths of the 3mm (⅛in) wide
black paper together end to end; use to make a loose closed coil and form
into a crescent. For the head, glue two 40cm (15¾in) lengths of the 3mm
(⅛in) wide black paper together end to end; make a loose closed coil and
pinch to make ears. Use 2mm (1/16in) wide paper strips to make tight coils for
the eyes and nose; insert. Cut and fix fine whisker strips. For the legs, make four very loose
closed coils from 20cm (8in) lengths of the 3mm (⅛in) wide black paper; pinch almost flat
at one end to a point. To maintain the leg shape, use a cocktail stick (toothpick) to place
glue inside the flat end of the coil, then press together, leaving the rounded end unglued.
Assemble the cat and glue to orange paper; add a tail. Secure behind the card aperture
and finish with the ribbon.

HAND-STITCHED STOCKING

It is the traditions, such as hanging up the stockings on Christmas Eve, that make Christmas so very special. This design brings the hand-stitched stockings of yesteryear bang up to date with the addition of colourful ribbons, button charms and a pompom trim in bright, contemporary colours. Three simple stitches are used to decorate – running stitch, cross stitch and straight stitch.

you will need

- orange single fold card 21 × 10cm (8¼ × 4in)
- white card
- pink paper
- orange handmade silk-fibre paper
- strips of pink handmade silk-fibre paper in three different shades
- orange ric-rac braid, narrow pink and orange grosgrain ribbons
- deep pink embroidery thread and size 22 embroidery needle
- fine-tip white gel pen
- embellishments – pompom trim; white, red and purple very narrow satin ribbons; buttons, assorted sizes, shapes and colours; heart-shaped gemstones

tip Handmade papers are supple enough to allow a needle to pass through easily but strong enough to withstand the handling.

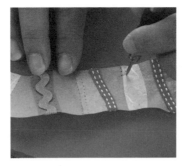

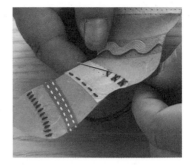

Step One Cut the stocking from the orange paper (see Templates). Glue the pink strips across the stocking, alternating the shades and leaving strips of the orange showing in between. Trim to the stocking outline. Cut the ribbons and ric-rac into 6cm (2³⁄₈in) lengths and stick on. Fold the ends of the ribbon under the stocking to avoid fraying.

Step Two Working on a foam mat, use a paper piercer to prick out guideline holes for the stitching. For running stitch, prick out a single line of regularly spaced holes about 2mm (³⁄₃₂in) from the paper strip edge. For cross stitch and straight stitch, prick out two parallel lines of holes, one resting on the paper strip edge and the other about 4mm (⁵⁄₃₂in) away.

Step Three Thread the needle with three strands of embroidery thread. Starting at the stocking toe, take the needle up from the back of the stocking and stitch neatly through the paper layers from edge to edge. As you complete each row, cut off the thread and tape the end securely to the back. Continue until you reach the stocking top.

Step Four Apply glue to the back of the stocking with a dry glue stick and fix to the white card; carefully smooth down flat to avoid pulling the stitching or ribbons. Cut around the shape leaving a 2mm (³⁄₃₂in) border of white card. Fix pompom trim to the top edge of the stocking.

Step Five Cut a piece of pink paper 18.5 × 8cm (7³⁄₈ × 3¹⁄₈in) and stick to the centre of the base card. Use the white gel pen to add a line of fake stitching around the edge. Place adhesive foam pads on the stocking back and fix it to the middle of the pink panel leaving an equal space at the top and bottom.

Step Six To decorate the buttons, thread narrow ribbon (or embroidery thread) through the buttonholes and tie in a knot or a bow; trim the ends diagonally. Use strong clear glue to fix the buttons on; add a further selection of heart-shaped gemstones and motif-style button charms.

tip For a hanging button charm, stack three buttons together in order of size (smallest on top); tie together with a narrow white ribbon. Glue to a circle of white card and fix on with a length of white ribbon.

Quick-to-Make Stockings

A die-cutting system may be relatively costly, but it's a great way to make cards in bulk.

you will need

- cream single fold card 14.5cm (5¾in) square
- white and burgundy card
- three complementary printed papers
- three wooden mini pegs
- very narrow green ribbon
- die-cutting tool and stocking die-cut
- heart punch
- beige sewing thread and sewing needle

Cut three stockings from printed papers and three from white card (see Techniques: Die-Cutting). Cut a burgundy card panel and mount onto a printed paper panel cut slightly larger; round off the corners. Attach to the base card. Use strong glue to fix the pegs to the mounted panel. Tie a knot at either end of a length of ribbon and thread through the pegs. Punch three hearts; using a needle, tie beige thread in a double knot and trim the ends; glue on.

Fun in the Snow

Embossing on vellum captures a frosty night by moonlight and adds texture to the bears' fur.

you will need

- blue single fold card 11 x 14.5 cm (4½ x 5¾in)
- white card
- polar bears and sleigh rubber stamp
- Mediterranean blue Brilliance™ inkpad
- plain vellum
- small circle punch
- two white eyelets

Stamp the image onto the vellum. When the ink is thoroughly dry, turn over and, working on a foam mat, use a fine ball embossing tool to draw on the bears' fur, a row of mountains above, and falling snowflakes. Cut a piece of vellum 11 x 14.5cm (4½ x 5¾in), and score and fold a flap 1.5cm (⅝in) wide along the top edge. Hook the flap over the top of the blue card and secure on the back. Tear a strip of white card and punch a white card circle. Arrange and glue in place under the vellum. Set the eyelets to secure the vellum panel to the card front.

Festive Fairy

This little fairy, springing from a sparkling snowflake backdrop, is wired for festive fun.

you will need

- white textured single fold card 15 x 10cm (6 x 4in)
- white textured card and small scallop-top tag
- snowflakes and fairy rubber stamps
- daisy punches
- blue and permanent black inkpads
- 22-gauge silver wire
- pale yellow, turquoise and bright blue shimmer paints
- blue crystals and glitter glue

Using the blue inkpad, randomly stamp snowflakes over the base card. Using the black inkpad, stamp the fairy onto white card. Colour in. Cut around the outline, cutting off the arms and legs. Cut out the hands and feet, and set aside. Fashion a halo from silver wire and attach to the back of the head with tape. Bend a short length of wire into a 'V' shape for arms, thread through slits cut on either side of the body; glue on the hands. Make two wire coils for the legs; glue on the feet; attach to the back of the dress. Punch out daisies and glue together for a garland; colour in. Glue crystals to the flower centres; fix to the fairy's hands. Fix the tag to the card; mount the fairy onto the tag with adhesive foam pads. Highlight with glitter glue.

Pretty Poinsettias

The poinsettia with its bright red flowers has become the traditional Christmas plant.

you will need

- red single fold card 15 x 10.5cm (6 x 4⅛in)
- green card
- watercolour paper
- poinsettia rubber stamp
- clear embossing inkpad
- red, green and brown inkpads
- white embossing powder
- yellow glaze pen
- narrow green organza ribbon

Stamp the poinsettia on the watercolour paper using the clear embossing inkpad; heat emboss using the white embossing powder; leave to dry. Use the colour inkpads to decorate the stamped flower. Use the yellow pen to add dots of colour to the flower centres. Once dry, trim and attach to a green card panel. Mount onto the base card. Tie ribbon around the spine.

SNOWMEN CASH CARD

Gift vouchers make ideal presents for family and friends who live far away. This super card has a slip-in pocket to hold a voucher and it can be enjoyed long after the voucher has been spent. Layering paper shapes onto the background card, which is then cut away to reveal the rubber-stamped panel beneath, creates the delightful snowmen figures.

tip To make a smaller holder for a credit-card style voucher, use a single forward-facing snowman.

you will need

- light blue card A4 (US letter) sheet
- white textured pearlescent card A4 (US letter) sheet
- pale blue and brown textured pearlescent card
- scraps of orange card and brilliant green paper
- snowflakes rubber stamp
- silver pigment inkpad
- pale blue and white opaque gel pens
- black and red gelly roll pens
- mid-blue brush marker pen
- small holly sprig punch

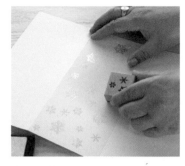

Step One Score the light blue card into three equal sections, concertina fold and open out flat. Randomly stamp silver snowflakes over the centre section. Use the gel pens to fill in any empty areas of the background with a dotted pattern. Re-fold the card so that the third facing you has the fold at its base.

Step Two Cut a piece of pale blue pearlescent card 3 × 21cm (1⅛ × 8¼in) into gently rolling hills and glue along the fold line to make the ground for the snowmen to stand on. Cut the body pieces from white pearlescent card (see Templates). Assemble the figures; position the largest body pieces close to the fold equally spaced.

Step Three Cut around the completed snowmen leaving a 6mm (¼in) border around the hills and an even narrower border around the figures. Run the side of a mid-blue brush marker pen along the cut edges of the outlines so that they stand out from the revealed stamped background.

Step Four Cut six twig arms (two of each) from the brown card and glue in place. To make the end figures look as if they are facing inwards, stick one arm to the back of each figure. Cut three small triangles of orange card for the carrot noses and glue in place. Add facial details and buttons with the black gelly roll pen.

Step Five Cut three hats from the brown card and decorate. Use the white opaque gel pen to mark on three rows of small dots for the hatband. Punch holly sprigs from the brilliant green paper, adding red gelly roll pen spots for the berries. When the ink is completely dry, glue the holly sprigs to the side of each hat.

Step Six Place a double thickness of adhesive foam tape above each snowman's head, leaving approximately 1mm (1/32in) clearance. Decide how to position the hats, and when you are happy press down firmly onto the tape. The hat brims keep the snowmen in place so that a voucher can be slipped behind.

tip Use the white pen to mark closely spaced dots on the hill border for freshly fallen snow.

Santa's Special Delivery

This card is ideal for presenting a gift of a plastic swipe card voucher. A triangular slot is cut into the front to hold a token.

you will need

- green single fold triangle card
- red, pink, black, white textured pearlescent card
- Christmas printed paper
- gold inkpad
- one large and two small paper fasteners

Use the gold inkpad to decorate the edges of the triangle card. Mark a triangular tab measuring 2.5cm (1in) in from the sides and the bottom. Open the card; cut along the marked lines. To make the large Santa decoration (see Templates), cut the base body and jacket from red card. Fix the jacket to the body with adhesive foam pads. Cut the fur trim from white pearlescent card. Cut the beard and curl the edges over a scissor blade. Fix to the front of the hood. Cut a pink circle and add the facial details; fix behind the hood. Add the black boots, gloves and belt, decorated with gold brads. Mount the figure on the tab.

Rudolph the Reindeer

Use pipe cleaners to fashion the antlers of a lovable reindeer – the tag can be removed from the card to hang on the tree.

you will need

- green single fold card 15 x 10cm (6 x 4in)
- brown and cream card
- brown and red felt
- two brown pipe cleaners
- red craft wire
- four silver and six gold bells
- two wiggly eyes

Cut the reindeer's head (see Templates) from white card, glue to the brown felt and trim. Glue on a red felt nose. Attach two wiggly eyes and draw on a mouth. Thread the silver bells onto 3cm (1⅛in) lengths of pipe cleaner. To make an antler, take one piece of pipe cleaner threaded with a bell and twist onto an 8cm (3⅛in) length of pipe cleaner; twist another short piece with a bell on just above the first. Cut a tag from a brown and cream card panel. Attach the antlers to the tag with double-sided tape. Place adhesive foam pads on the back of the head and attach over the ends of the antlers. To finish thread on a length of red wire decorated with gold bells.

Gingerbread Man

This shaped design is quick to make by folding card in half and cutting out the front and back in one go.

you will need

- brown card A4 (US letter) sheet
- brown inkpad (darker than the card)
- white 3D paint and black glaze pen
- very narrow red ribbon

Fold the brown card in half. Make a gingerbread man card template (see Templates), and use to draw around onto one side of the folded card (ensure the end of one arm butts up to the fold, as this needs to remain uncut). Cut out. Sponge around the edges of the card, back and front, with a sponge dipped into the inkpad. Decorate with white 3D paint. Add black button eyes and a bright red bow to finish.

tip Draw around a gingerbread man cookie cutter if you have one.

Advent Card

This card helps to count down the last few days before Christmas. It's a great way to use up those leftover pieces of card and decorative materials from other card projects.

you will need

- green single fold card 15cm (6in) square
- green card and scraps of coloured card
- embroidery threads and embroidery needle
- number peel-off stickers
- seven Christmas themed stickers
- seven coloured brads
- tag punch

Punch six tags from coloured card. Make a hole in the top of each and use a needle to thread through hanging bows. Decorate the tag fronts with numbers 19 to 24, and the reverse with the stickers. Make a larger tag from red card; decorate the front with a large 25, and use your most special sticker for the back. Insert the brads through the card front and loop a tag onto each; hide the brad 'legs' inside the card with a green card panel.

55

BY CANDLELIGHT

Candles symbolize hope and love at Christmas-time. Floral decorations make a fitting accompaniment, here quickly and cleverly recreated in paper using the technique of fringed quilling (see Techniques: Quilling). Holly leaves grouped around the sparkly flowers are scored and shaped to give a naturalistic 3D effect. Parchment-backed apertures permit suffused light to highlight the candles framed within.

you will need

- purple single fold card 14cm (5½in) square
- yellow and dark green card
- parchment paper
- red and purple metallic 1cm (³/8in) wide paper strip
- fringing tool
- quilling tool

Step One Open out the base card and place, wrong side up, on a cutting mat. Measure and mark out three apertures 2cm (¾in), 3cm (1⅛in) and 2cm (¾in) wide by 9cm (3½in) high; cut out. Place double-sided tape all around and on either side of the central aperture. Remove the backing. Fix a piece of parchment paper on top.

Step Two Turn the card over. Cut three 7cm (2¾in) lengths of red paper strip. Cut a curve in the tops and trim the lengths to graduate in size. Attach one to each parchment panel, tucking the strip ends under the purple card. Cut three flames from yellow card. Colour the centres with an orange felt-tip pen.

Step Three Use the holly leaf template (see Templates) to cut six leaves from the dark green card. Place one holly leaf on a cutting mat. Using a small ball embossing tool, score a line down the centre and then small lines outwards from the central line. Use your fingers to curl the leaf slightly. Repeat with the other leaves.

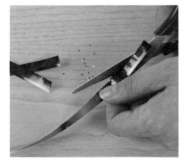

Step Four Run two 40cm (15¾in) lengths of purple paper strip, metallic side down, through the fringing tool. Cut four 15cm (6in) lengths of the fringed paper. Trim about 2mm (³⁄₃₂in) off the fringed edge to make the flowers a little smaller.

Step Five Insert one end of a fringed length of paper through the prongs of a quilling tool. Rotate the tool, making sure that the metallic side is facing inwards.

Step Six Continue rotating until the end of the paper is reached, then apply a dot of PVA (white) glue to the end. Hold against the coil for a few seconds while the glue dries. Spread out the fringes with your fingers. Repeat with the other fringed lengths. Attach the leaves and the flowers in the top left- and bottom right-hand corners.

tip As an alternative to the holly leaf template, you could use a punch or die-cut.

We Three Kings

This is a quick to make luxury card that beautifully portrays the journey of the three kings to Bethlehem.

you will need

- 🌿 purple single fold card 15 x 10cm (6 x 4in)
- 🌿 rainbow paper
- 🌿 black three kings outline peel-off sticker
- 🌿 gold star and diamond peel-off stickers

Place the three kings peel-off sticker on the rainbow paper and cut out. Glue centrally to the front of the single fold card. Add diamond, stars, and one large star peel-off to the desert sky. Border the card with a large star peel-off in each corner, positioning diamond peel-offs in between.

Hanging Bauble

An ultra-quick card for those who have little time to spare for their card making on the run up to Christmas.

you will need

- 🌿 light purple textured single fold card 12 cm (4¾in) square with circular aperture
- 🌿 dark purple card
- 🌿 silver large bauble outline peel-off sticker
- 🌿 silver cord

Stick the bauble peel-off sticker to the dark purple card and cut out around the outside edge. Working on a foam mat, echo the bauble's design with a pattern pricked with a single-needle pricking tool. Carefully cut away the card from the bauble's hanging loop and use silver cord to hang from the single fold card's circular aperture.

Let It Snow

Rubber stamped snowmen peer out from a snowy wonderland from inside this shaker card.

you will need
- purple single fold card 15cm (6in) square
- two pieces of white card 13.7cm (5½in) square
- self-adhesive foam 13.7cm (5½in) square
- acetate 13.7cm (5½in) square
- snowmen and snowflakes rubber stamps
- lilac pigment inkpad
- black waterproof dye inkpad
- pastel brush markers
- glitter glue
- rock salt and fine glitter

Cut a round aperture from one of the white card squares; decorate with a snowflakes stamp and add sparkle in between with dots of glitter glue. Lightly trace the aperture onto the second piece of white card. Stamp snowmen within the pencilled circle; colour with the marker pens. Stick the snowmen panel centrally on the purple card. Stick the foam square to align with the snowmen panel. Fill the shaker well with rock salt and glitter. Stick the acetate to the back of the snowflake panel. Remove the backing strips from the shaker box and glue the snowflake panel on top.

Crowning Glory

This crown aperture card, topped with gems made from closed quilled coils, is so simple to make.

you will need
- purple single fold card 15 x 10cm (6 x 4in)
- red, green and purple card
- gold-edged red 3mm (⅛in) wide quilling paper strips
- quilling tool
- gold pen

Using the crown templates (see Templates) cut the larger crown from green card and the smaller crown from purple card and stick together. Mark the crown outline on the front of the purple single fold card and cut out. Use the gold pen to outline both the aperture and the small purple crown. Attach a panel of red card to the inside back. Close the card and lightly mark the outline of the crown aperture onto the red card. Open the card and glue the layered crown onto the marked crown outline. Make three closed coil 'gems' and glue on.

Life's Special Moments

This section is packed full of card designs to help you to celebrate all the most important events in the lives of your family and friends, from a young couple's engagement to a ruby wedding anniversary, from a child's first day at school to someone's happy retirement.

Wedding congratulations, birth announcements, exam successes – there are so many reasons to make a handmade greeting. The exciting designs featured include a luxurious collage wedding invitation, a stencilled key coming of age card, and a pocket card for those about to embark on a trip of a lifetime to store their memories.

Whatever the occasion you will find the perfect design to mark the event.

HEARTS AND FLOWERS

A handmade engagement card is the perfect way to congratulate a
happy couple. Gold hearts symbolize love and a sprinkling of tiny glass
beads give a luxurious finish to this stunning card. A multiple aperture
card blank is used, with both surface and see-through embellishments.
A coordinating envelope is the perfect finish to this special greeting.

you will need

♡ **coral single fold
   card with nine
   apertures 14.8cm
   (5¾in) square**

♡ **five gold metal
   hearts**

♡ **clear sticky squares
   and daisy peel-off
   stickers**

♡ **double-sided
   adhesive paper A4
   (US letter) sheet**

♡ **coral-mix micro
   beads and self-seal
   plastic bag**

♡ **flower punch**

♡ **envelope**

Step One Working on a plastic surface and from the inside of the card, place a clear sticky square over the middle aperture. Place clear sticky squares over the apertures above, below and to each side of the centre aperture to form a cross shape.

Step Two Turn the card over and position a gold heart in the middle of the centre square and firm down really well, so that the beads cannot get underneath it. Position a daisy sticker in the centre of each of the surrounding four squares and firm down well.

Step Three Place the micro beads into the self-seal bag. Push the card into the bag and use your fingers to rub the beads over the top of the sticky squares. Shake off any excess beads and remove the card.

Step Four Close the card and apply a dot of dimensional glue to the centre of each of the remaining squares, on the inside of the card. Pick up the gold hearts and stick one in the centre of each of the squares. Leave to dry.

Step Five Punch out three flowers from double-sided adhesive paper. Peel-off one side of the backing paper and position the flowers down the left-hand side of the envelope, leaving plenty of room for the address. Remove the top backing paper.

Step Six Place the envelope in the bag and rub the beads over the daisy shapes. Shake off any excess beads and remove the envelope.

tip Lick your finger to help you pick up each individual gold heart more easily.

The Happy Couple

This engagement party invitation card has a decorative insert that lifts out to reveal the happy couple romantically framed.

you will need
♡ white card 16 x 23cm (6¼ x 9in)
♡ polka dot card 14.5 x 10 cm (5¾ x 4in)
♡ pink and striped printed paper
♡ photographs of the happy couple

Make an envelope from the white card. Cover with the pink and striped printed paper. Using the heart template (see Templates), draw two hearts on the envelope front. Open out and cut out the hearts. Crop the photos to fit and stick on the inside. Punch a semicircle in the centre top edge of the front panel. Assemble the envelope. Punch a hole at the top of the polka dot card and thread ribbon through. Write or print on the back and insert into the envelope.

A Gem of a Card

This little card decorated with a sparkling quilled ring, set with a gemstone, is a unique way to celebrate an engagement.

Layer a cream card square onto a slightly larger orange card square and stick to the front of the pink single fold card. Wrap a 30cm (12in) length paper strip around the handle of a wooden spoon. Put a dot of glue on the end of the paper, wrap the paper around the handle, not too tightly, and press to the glue so that the rings of paper are exactly in line. Continue to wind the paper around the handle until the end is reached (see Techniques: Quilling). Make a loose closed coil with a 10cm (4in) length. Pinch into a square shape and glue to the ring at the join. Glue the gemstone on the square coil.

you will need
♡ pink single fold card 6 x 5cm (2¼ x 2in)
♡ orange and cream card
♡ gold-edged ivory 3mm (1/8in) wide quilling paper strips
♡ quilling tool
♡ clear gemstone

tip If you don't have a gemstone, add silver glitter glue to the top of the square coil.

Perfect Proposal

The happy couple can celebrate their special moment with this romantic yet cute cat stamp.

you will need

- ♡ purple single fold card 10cm (4in) square
- ♡ white card
- ♡ light lilac paper heart
- ♡ cat couple rubber stamp
- ♡ black inkpad
- ♡ brush markers
- ♡ narrow pink sheer ribbon

Glue the paper heart to the centre of the purple single fold card. Stamp the cats onto a piece of white card and roughly cut around their outline; colour with brush markers. Mount the stamped panel in the centre of the heart with adhesive foam pads. Wrap the ribbon around the card and tie in a bow to one side.

Heartfelt Wishes

This is a super-quick card that can be made in minutes for when a couple's announcement takes you by surprise.

you will need

- ♡ cream single fold card 12cm (4¾in) square
- ♡ purple self-adhesive vellum
- ♡ heart punch
- ♡ narrow purple sheer ribbon
- ♡ three mini tags

Cut a strip of the self-adhesive vellum and stick to the centre of the cream single fold card. Punch three vellum hearts and stick to the tags. Add beautiful sheer ribbon to finish the look, and attach the tags with adhesive foam pads.

WEDDING BOUQUET

This luxurious wedding card uses a tri-fold card to maximize the space available for decoration. Die-cut rosebuds adorn the left-hand panel, a beribboned heart provides the focus for the centre panel, and to the right three classic wedding images have been stamped and embossed on vellum to build up delicate layers. The overall effect is highly decorative yet subtle.

you will need

- ❧ white textured card 18 x 21cm (7 x 8¼in)
- ❧ red, green and silver card
- ❧ plain vellum
- ❧ pearl embossed paper
- ❧ hearts, bouquet and champagne glasses rubber stamps
- ❧ rocket red Brilliance™ inkpad
- ❧ large square frame punch
- ❧ die-cutting tool and heart and rosebud dies
- ❧ narrow white satin ribbon

Step One Stamp the designs twice on vellum. Place one of the bouquet images right side down and fill in the flowers, stems, ribbon and frill. Draw spot clusters around the bouquet. Repeat with the second bouquet, but only emboss the frill and flowers. Prepare the hearts and glasses in the same way, but use crosses around the hearts and wavy lines around the glasses.

Step Two Carefully cut out the overlapping hearts, glasses tops and bases, and bouquet flowers and frill from the less decorated images. Apply tiny dots of tacky craft glue to the edges of the bouquet. Stick directly on top of the whole bouquet image. Repeat with the glasses and hearts.

Step Three Punch three square frames from red card. Cut out the frames using scissors, as they remain attached to the card. Trim off the notches remaining on the sides of the punched frames.

Step Four Mount the vellum squares on the frames – apply tiny dots of Hi-Tack Glue™ to the corners of the vellum, then press down until the glue begins to set.

Step Five Score the white textured card to create three panels; concertina fold. Cut two pieces of pearl embossed paper 18 x 8cm (7 x 3¼in); tear down one side of each piece and stick in place over the concertina fold. Die-cut the three rosebuds from red and green card, assemble and mount, overlapping the torn edge of paper on the left-hand panel.

Step Six Mount the three framed vellum squares, overlapping the torn edge of paper on the right-hand panel. Die-cut a heart tag from silver card and thread onto the ribbon. Wrap the ribbon around the centre panel and tie in a bow.

tip Allow a little longer for the ink to dry on vellum. If necessary, use a heat gun to speed up the process.

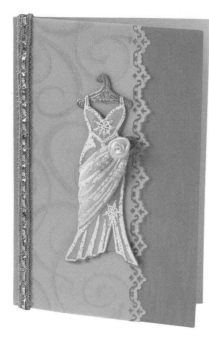

Bridal Dress

This elegant yet contemporary stamped and layered card is a perfect memento of the big day.

you will need

- silver single fold card 15 x 10cm (6 x 4in)
- silver card
- white vellum and scroll-printed vellum with lace effect border
- dress on hanger rubber stamp
- VersaMark™ inkpad
- white and silver embossing powders
- embellishments – silver ribbon, satin rosebud and pearl bead string

Stamp the dress onto white vellum twice and heat emboss with white embossing powder. Use silver embossing powder to heat emboss a third dress on silver card. Cut all three out: leave the silver image whole; cut the hanger from one and discard; cut and retain the sash from the other. Lay the vellum pieces face down in your palm; gently rub with an embossing tool in a circular motion until the vellum begins to curl. Use silicone adhesive to assemble the dress; leave to dry. Layer the scroll-printed vellum strip and dress onto the card, and add embellishments to finish.

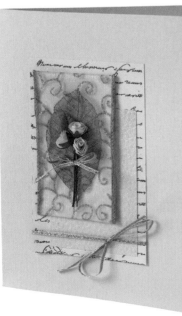

Wedding Invitation

A rich cream and gold palette is used to produce this exquisite collage card.

you will need

- white single fold card 18 x 13cm (7 x 5in)
- cream embossed card
- manuscript printed paper
- gold skeleton leaf
- three paper rosebuds
- wide gold patterned ribbon
- narrow gold ribbon

Layer the panels of manuscript printed paper, cream embossed card and gold patterned ribbon backed by a piece of white card; tie a length of the narrow ribbon around the bottom of the layered panel. Stick centrally onto the front of the white single fold card. Use tacky craft glue to stick the skeleton leaf carefully onto the ribbon. Tie the paper roses with the remaining narrow ribbon and stick onto the skeleton leaf to finish.

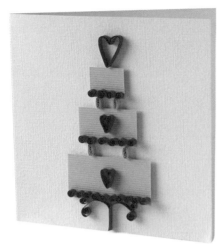

Wedding Cake Congratulations

This fabulous quilled wedding cake design makes for a lovely wedding acceptance card.

you will need

- white single fold card 10cm (4in) square
- pink textured card
- quilling tool
- copper-edged dusty pink, brown and light pink 3mm (¹⁄₈in) wide quilling paper strips

Make two small and one large heart, and ten open 'S' coils (scrolls) from the copper-edged pink paper (see Techniques: Quilling for details). Make four tier posts from 7cm (2¾in) lengths of light pink paper strips formed into loose closed coils and pinched into rectangles. For the cake tiers, use mini adhesive foam pads to mount three pink card rectangles onto the base card ascending in size. Glue the tier posts in between the top two tiers, and scrolls along the bottom edges. Stick on the hearts. For the cake stand, fold a 10cm (4in) length of the brown paper in half, then open out. Apply glue for 3cm (1¹⁄₈in) to one side of the fold. Fold over and press down, so that the paper is glued double but the ends are free. Using the quilling tool, coil each end outwards, and glue in place.

Contemporary Wedding

A bold, graphic stamp design of the bridal couple is enhanced by a striking colour scheme of whites, greys and blacks.

you will need

- white single fold card 16 x 11cm (6¼ x 4¼in)
- smooth white and black card
- black and grey striped printed paper
- bride and groom rubber stamp
- graphite black Brilliance™ inkpad
- black and clear gems
- silver thread

Stamp the bride and groom design onto smooth white card; use a brush to shade in the bouquet roses. Trim the card to 13.5 x 8cm (5¼ x 3¼in) and mount on a slightly larger piece of black card. Cover the single fold card with the striped paper. Mount the panel onto the card and add a black gem to each corner. Add clear gems to the groom's shirt front and the bride's ear. Tie a length of silver thread in a bow and glue below the floral bouquet.

LOVING BEARS

This delightful stamp featuring two cuddly bears strolling arm-in-arm is perfect for celebrating a wedding anniversary. Here, a bleaching technique has been used to create the impression of fur on the stamped bears. Bleach is painted on to remove varying degrees of colour from dark-coloured card to create a textural effect.

you will need

- ✂ cream hammer-textured single fold card 14.5cm (5¾in) square
- ✂ brown and tan card
- ✂ scraps of light yellow and white textured card
- ✂ bear couple with posy rubber stamp
- ✂ VersaMark™ inkpad
- ✂ clear embossing powder
- ✂ thick bleach
- ✂ die-cutting tool and large oval die
- ✂ four gold brads
- ✂ small flower punch

Step One
Using the VersaMark™ inkpad, stamp the image onto brown card. Sprinkle a thin layer of clear embossing powder all over the image. Tip off the excess, then return it to the jar.

Step Two
Heat the surface of the embossing powder with a heat gun (see Techniques: Heat Embossing). Make sure that all the powder has melted and that the outline of the bears has raised. Don't overheat the powder, as the lines will sink and appear oily.

Step Three
Protect your work surface with scrap paper. Pour a small quantity of bleach into a jar. Using a fine paintbrush and clean water, dilute a little of the bleach and paint onto the bears in small strokes, leaving some areas untouched. Paint the bouquet entirely with bleach.

Step Four
Leave to dry. You can speed up the drying with the heat gun, but avoid overheating the embossing. Apply more bleach if you need to lighten some areas further. Paint strokes of bleach around the bears' feet to create the ground.

Step Five
Colour in the bouquet and leave to dry.

Step Six
To finish, die-cut an oval aperture in a piece of tan card 13.5 x 12cm (5¼ x 4¾in). Glue to the bleached panel to frame the bears. Mount on the single fold card. Punch holes in the corners with a 1.5mm (1/16in) hole punch and insert brads. Punch small yellow flowers and white centres; assemble and stick on at random.

tip In order to control the shading and to achieve a variety of tones, allow each application of bleach a few minutes to work to gauge the full effect before applying further layers.

Ruby Wedding

A simple card decorated with a dried red rose celebrates the achievement of 40 years of marriage.

you will need
- cream single fold card 15 x 10cm (6 x 4in)
- red and cream card
- dried red rose
- narrow white sheer ribbon

Mount a red card panel and a slightly smaller cream card panel onto the single fold card. Tie the sheer ribbon in a bow around the stem of the dried red rose and stick securely to the mounted panel.

tip For added interest a corner punch has been used for the cream card panel.

Anniversary Greetings

A luxurious beaded heart has been fashioned to decorate a simple ribbon-decorated card ideal for any anniversary.

you will need
- white single fold card 15 x 10cm (6 x 4in)
- seed or bugle beads
- 22-gauge wire
- round-nosed pliers
- wide burgundy sheer ribbon

Cut a 24cm (9½in) length of wire and use the round-nosed pliers to shape a hook that will stop the beads coming off. Thread seed or bugle beads on to cover completely and fashion into a heart shape. Wrap the ribbon down the front of the card and secure on the reverse with double-sided tape. Carefully apply PVA (white) glue to the back of the beaded heart and mount on the ribbon. Put a heavy weight on top and leave to dry for at least 30 minutes.

Silver Wedding

Toast the happy couple with champagne to celebrate 25 years of marriage.

you will need

- ✂ silver single fold card 15cm (6in) square
- ✂ light and dark silver card
- ✂ silver vellum
- ✂ champagne glasses rubber stamp
- ✂ silver embossing inkpad
- ✂ silver embossing powder
- ✂ large, medium and small silver peel-off heart stickers
- ✂ narrow silver ribbon

Cut a 15 x 9cm (6 x 3⁵⁄₈in) panel of vellum, fold in 2cm (¾in) and secure to the back of the folded edge of the card with double-sided tape. Stamp and emboss the champagne glasses onto a dark silver card panel and mount onto a light silver card panel cut slightly larger. Mount the stamped panel half on the vellum and half on the card using adhesive foam pads. Decorate the vellum panel with the hearts. To finish, add three small hearts to the bottom right-hand corner and tie a ribbon bow on the folded edge.

Golden Wedding

A golden wedding anniversary, demands a very special card such as this gold embossed shaker card.

you will need

- ✂ large gold single fold card
- ✂ cream and gold card
- ✂ acetate
- ✂ wedding cake rubber stamp
- ✂ gold embossing inkpad
- ✂ eight filigree corner embellishments
- ✂ small gold heart sequins

Cut a rectangular aperture in a gold card panel cut about 1.3cm (½in) smaller all around than your single fold card. Securely fix the filigree corner embellishments in place. Trace lightly through the aperture onto a cream card background. Stamp and emboss a wedding cake in gold within the pencilled frame. Make up the shaker, filling it with small gold heart sequins, and then mount onto the card.

TEDDY TWINS

This versatile design works just as well for a birth announcement or to celebrate a birth – perhaps even for twins! The cutting technique instantly turns an ordinary stamped design into a great novelty card, but as the outline of the stamped image – the teddies' fur – is difficult to cut around, a simplified cutting line is drawn a short distance away from the image.

you will need

- white card 10.5 x 14.8cm (4¼ x 5½in)
- pearlescent sky blue Brilliance™ inkpad
- teddies and paw print rubber stamps
- light blue gel pen
- three small, light blue buttons
- narrow white satin ribbon

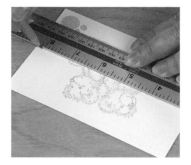

Step One Stamp the teddies centrally on the white card and a paw print in each bottom corner. Mark the halfway point on one short side of the card and make a small mark. Repeat on the other short side. Draw a line between the two points as softly as possible and avoid drawing on the teddies.

Step Two Using the line going across the card as the starting and finishing point, draw a soft pencil line around the top half of the teddies, 3–4mm (⅛in) away from them and loosely following the outline of the heads – if the line is too wiggly, it will be difficult to cut.

Step Three Place the card on a cutting mat. Again using the line going across the middle as the starting and finishing point, cut along the pencil line and around the teddies with a craft knife. Keep the cutting action as smooth as possible. Erase all the pencil lines and marks.

tip To attach the buttons use strong, flexible PVA (white) glue dabbing on with a cocktail stick (toothpick) for precision.

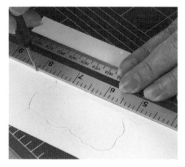

Step Four Turn the card over and mark the halfway points as in Step 1. Use the fine ball on a dual embossing tool to score a line between the points on either side of the teddies. Use the cut line to see where to start and finish.

Step Five Using a wet paintbrush, pick up some ink from the inkpad. Shade the teddies with soft layers of the ink. Keep the shading on the outer edges of the arms, legs and heads. This will give the teddies a 3D look.

Step Six Make sure that the cut line around the teddies has no sections left uncut before carefully folding back the upper half of the card. Fold the card into the crease scored along the back. Use a gel pen to draw a stitched line across the card on either side just beneath the fold. Attach a ribbon bow in between the teddies and glue on the buttons

Newborn Pram

Transform a small square card into a baby's pram with this novelty design to celebrate a little boy's birth.

you will need

- white single fold card 13cm (5$\frac{1}{8}$in) square
- white card
- blue printed papers
- wavy-edged scissors
- thin blue satin ribbon

tip To finish add a silver punched heart decorated as you wish.

Trace off the newborn pram template (see Templates) onto the front of the card using a soft pencil and cut out. Cover the front with blue printed paper. Fold strips of a second printed paper into pleats and glue along the edges of the pram. Use the wavy-edged scissors to cut along one edge of two white card strips measuring 1.5 x 8cm (½ x 3$\frac{1}{8}$in) each. Glue over the pleats and stick ribbon on top.

Baby's Here

Small tags decorated with baby embellishments are a great way to announce baby's arrival as details such as birth weight and date can be added to the back of each tag.

Cover the front of the card with spotted paper. Cut five 2.5cm (1in) diameter circles from the beige card. Fix an eyelet near the edge of each circle and decorate with an embellishment. Stick a piece of ribbon along the card 1.5cm (½in) from the fold. Loop each tag on a 4cm (1½in) length of ribbon and stick the ends to the ribbon at the top of the card so that the tags hang down; hide the join with small ribbon bows.

you will need

- cream single fold card 7 x 18.5cm (2¾ x 7¼in)
- beige card
- spotted paper
- five eyelets
- baby theme embellishments
- very narrow white ribbon

Ducks in a Row

Cute little duck embellishments made from shrink plastic are used to decorate this sweet little card.

you will need

- pale green single fold card 15 x 10cm (6 x 4in)
- yellow and white card
- baby handprint paper
- shrink plastic and yellow acrylic paint
- thin yellow and narrow light green satin ribbon

Cut three large and five small yellow ducks from shrink plastic (see Templates). Heat following the manufacturer's instructions and allow to cool before painting. Cut a piece of patterned paper slightly smaller than the card front and stick in place. Using the bib template, cut out a yellow card back and a white card front and assemble on the base card. Decorate with yellow ribbon bows and the large ducks. Stick on the green ribbon and decorate with a row of small ducks.

tip Cut just inside the lines when cutting out the shrink plastic to avoid picking up the pen colour.

Welcome Baby Boy

This birth congratulations card, decorated with a combination of rubber stamp motifs and cute novelty buttons, would be perfect for the arrival of triplets.

you will need

- pale blue single fold card 15 x 10cm (6 x 4in)
- small mid-blue card squares
- printed papers
- baby-grow and nappy (diaper) pin rubber stamps
- light blue inkpad
- black permanent inkpad
- baby theme embellishments

Using the light blue ink, stamp the single fold card with a background of nappy (diaper) pins. Using the black ink, stamp three baby grows onto printed papers of your choice; cut out. Securely glue a baby theme embellishment to each small card square. Mount the stamped baby-grows and button panels onto the card.

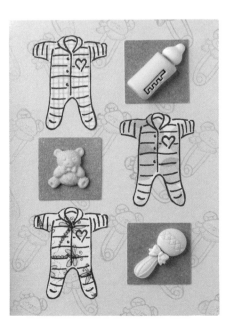

TEDDY BEAR CONCERTINA

The birth of new baby is a very special occasion and, as a treasured memento of the event, a photograph of the newborn is hidden within the miniature concertina card that adorns this lovely design. A daisy sticker has been used to create a stencilled background for the main card, and although elaborately decorated, this design is so easy to assemble.

you will need

- 🧸 pink single fold card 15 x 10cm (6 x 4in)
- 🧸 pink card 6.5 x 30cm (2⅝ x 11¾in)
- 🧸 pink Brilliance™ inkpad
- 🧸 floral pattern rubber stamp
- 🧸 daisy punch
- 🧸 pink micro beads and self-seal plastic bag
- 🧸 baby photograph
- 🧸 daisy and silver daisy panel peel-off stickers
- 🧸 clear sticky square
- 🧸 two pink flat back crystals
- 🧸 heart and teddy bear buttons
- 🧸 pink embroidery thread
- 🧸 very narrow pink ribbon

Step One Place a daisy peel-off sticker anywhere on the front of the pink single fold card. Use a sponge to carefully apply ink around the daisy. Lift the sticker and move to another part of the card and repeat. Sponge daisy motifs randomly across the front of the card.

Step Two Use an embossing tool and ruler to score at 5cm (2in) intervals across the length of the pink card strip, and then fold into a concertina booklet. Open out and work on the far right panel. Cut an aperture to frame the photograph you are using. Stamp the floral pattern around the frame's edges.

Step Three On the front of the booklet – the first panel on the left – stamp the floral pattern in the centre of the panel.

Step Four On the second panel, slide a daisy punch down from the top and punch out the shape. Turn over and stick a clear sticky square over the punched daisy. Put the micro beads into the self-seal bag. Slide in the strip and use your fingers to firm the beads onto the sticky daisy. Shake the excess beads back into the bag and remove.

Step Five Stencil a daisy pattern all over the third panel (see Step 1). Stick the daisy panel peel-off sticker in the centre. Add flat back crystals to the daisy centres with dimensional glue. Thread a strand of embroidery thread through the heart-shaped button and tie in a bow. Attach to the centre of the fourth panel with double-sided tape. Stick the teddy button to the stamped front panel.

Step Six Stick the photograph to the inside back page of the concertina using double-sided tape. Fold up and use double-sided tape to stick the pink ribbon to the back (so that you will be able to tie the ends in a bow at the front). Position the concertina on the front of the larger card; remove the tape backing and stick in place.

Welcome Baby Girl

Stamped polymer clay produces an effect rather like a cast of a baby's handprints, and makes a perfect congratulatory card for new parents.

you will need

- white single fold card 10 x 15cm (4 x 6in)
- assorted and yellow papers
- handprints and baby motifs border rubber stamps
- VersaMark™ inkpad
- pink embossing powder
- white polymer clay
- two heart buttons
- wavy-edged scissors
- narrow pink ribbon

Make a handprint cast from polymer clay (see Techniques: Stamping). Heat emboss the baby border design along a paper strip. Decorate the front of the card with pink paper panels and glue the paper strip on top. Cut a yellow paper strip with wavy-edged scissors and glue down the left-hand side. Stick the ribbon on top. Glue the handprints onto gingham paper, then onto yellow paper with a hand-torn edge and glue onto the base card. Attach the buttons to finish.

Cute as a Button

This cute teddy bear button decoration is made by stamping the design onto shrink plastic.

you will need

- white single fold card 12cm (4¾in) square
- white linen-effect card
- pink checked and spotted printed papers
- teddy bear rubber stamp
- coral Brilliance™ inkpad
- white shrink plastic
- jumbo scalloped square punch
- two pink brads
- white embroidery thread

Stamp the bear onto the shrink plastic, and use a cotton bud to decorate with coral ink spots. Once dry, cut out and punch two holes in the bear's tummy with a 3mm (1/8in) hole punch before shrinking. Punch a scalloped square from white card and cut a slightly smaller square from pink checked paper to glue on top. Decorate the front of the base card with a pink spotted paper panel and checked paper strip. Mount the scalloped panel over the strip with adhesive foam pads and attach a brad on either side of it. Mount the finished teddy bear button with an adhesive foam pad.

Quick Baby Bunny

An adorable 3D rabbit sticker makes the perfect centrepiece for this quick-to-make card.

Cut a 15 x 10cm (6 x 4in) panel of vellum, fold over 1cm (³⁄₈in) and secure to the back folded edge of the card with double-sided tape. Place the rabbit sticker in the centre of an 8 x 7cm (3¹⁄₈ x 2¾in) piece of cream card. Put a brad in each corner, and stick the cream panel to the centre of the card using double-sided tape.

you will need
- soft green single fold card 15cm (6in) square
- cream card
- soft toys embossed vellum
- 3D rabbit sticker
- four green daisy brads

tip To ensure the brads lay flat without marking the card, place the card right side up and push down on the daisies to flatten the legs out at the back.

New Baby on Board

There is no better way to announce the arrival of a new member to the family than with this timeless baby image – the pram.

Cut the pram body and hood from two different shades of pink card (see Templates). Punch five equally spaced holes on the pram body; fix to a light pink square of card using mini adhesive foam pads. Using a cocktail stick (toothpick), apply a dot of glue inside the punched holes onto the card below. Make loose coils and insert in the holes, letting the coils unwind to fit. Pinch five loose closed coils into crescent shapes and fix on the underside of the pram hood and above the pram body. Make tight coils for the wheels. Add legs, a strut and a handle to finish the pram. Mount the panel onto the base card.

you will need
- pink single fold card 10cm (4in) square
- pink card in three shades
- white and pink 3mm (¹⁄₈in) wide quilling paper strips
- quilling tool
- 7mm (¼in) 'anywhere' hole punch

DESIGNER HOME

New home owners are often keen to redecorate. Appropriately, a paint chart from a DIY store has inspired this design. The card, inkpad and paint chart have been beautifully colour coordinated. The graphic outline of the house works well against the blocks of colour and may even give the new home owners some interior design ideas.

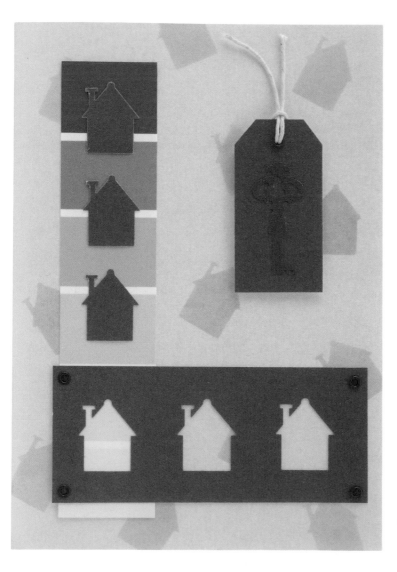

you will need

- cream single fold card 21 x 14.8cm (8¼ x 5¾in)
- fern green and antique gold card
- pearlized green inkpad
- house and key punches
- paint chart strip
- five green eyelets
- string

Step One Punch a house from a piece of scrap card to make a stencil. Sponge house motifs onto the front of the card. Position the houses randomly and let them spill over the edges of the card to give a more professional finish.

Step Two Insert the green card into the house punch, pushing the paper to the very back. For the second house line the edge of the punch up with the edge of the first punched out house. Repeat again to give a row of three houses; trim to a border strip with a craft knife and metal ruler

Step Three Cut a six-colour strip from the paint chart and stick to the front left of the stencilled card with double-sided tape. Glue the three punched out houses over the top four squares.

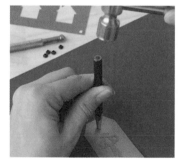

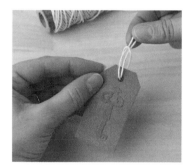

Step Four Cut a 7 x 3.5cm (2¾ x 1⅜in) piece of green card, trim the top corners to make a tag and punch a small hole at the top. Punch the key shapes from the gold card. Cut around the key shape you want to use (this particular punch creates three different keys at once), and stick to the tag using a glue pen. Leave to dry for a few minutes.

Step Five Position the punched house panel across the bottom of the card, overlapping the paint chart on the left; use an eyelet punch and hammer to make a hole through all layers in each corner of the panel and add eyelets to each hole. Make a hole and add an eyelet to the tag. Turn the tag and punched house panel over and use the setter tool and hammer to flatten the eyelets.

Step Six Cut a length of string and thread through the tag, making a loop at the front and pulling the ends through. Attach the tag to the top right of the card using adhesive foam pads.

Welcome to Your New Home

This card is the perfect size to accompany a new home gift for new neighbours.

Decorate the front of the card with the printed papers. Punch the tags from scraps of coloured cards to match the papers you have chosen. Stamp moving home images onto scraps of white card; cut out and colour in. Decorate the tags with the stamped images; for the centre tag, use a brad to attach a tag to it that has been decorated with a punch out heart and a key charm embellishment. Thread the tags onto ribbon and use mini pegs to hold them in place.

you will need

- small white single fold card
- striped and floral printed papers
- moving home rubber stamp
- tag and heart punch
- key charm and mini pegs
- thin gold ribbon

House Keys

Add house keys with a number tag to match that of your new house and you have the perfect change of address card.

Place the sapphire blue card right side up on the embossing board and, using an embossing tool, trace over the house pattern. Cut slits in the corners and put the legs of the brads through; turn over and open out flat. Mount on blue pearlized card and trim to leave a small border showing. Fix to the base card using double-sided tape. Punch two keys from silver card and add a peel-off sticker eyelet. Add an eyelet peel-off sticker and numbers to the tag; thread onto the chain and lock the ends together; mount on the card using adhesive foam pads.

you will need

- cream single fold card 15cm (6in) square with border
- sapphire blue card 7 x 11cm (2¾ x 5⁷⁄₈in)
- blue pearlized and silver card
- house embossing board and tool
- key punch
- four silver square brads
- black eyelet and numbers peel-off stickers
- metal tag and ball chain

The Recycled Home

This new home card uses the lining side of old business envelopes to provide the colour.

you will need

- dark blue single fold card 15 x 10cm (6 x 4in)
- white card
- scraps of blue printed papers

Use the house template to cut six houses (three of two different patterns) and six roofs (see Templates). Cut six 4cm (1½in) squares (three of two different patterns). Stick each house centrally on a contrasting square; add the roofs. Cut rectangles for windows, matching their colour with that of the background squares and stick these on. Arrange the houses, chequerboard style, on top of a rectangle of white card and stick centrally on the front of the base card.

tip You can iron old or used papers on a medium setting to get rid of any creases before you begin.

Home Sweet Home

Give a warm welcome to a new home with this pretty-as-a-picture house.

you will need

- house-shaped card blank
- pink, cream and coloured card
- diamond printed paper
- pink inkpad
- flower punch
- flat back crystals

Cover the roof of the house-shaped blank with diamond printed paper, cutting out the bottom row of diamonds and curling up by running along the blade of a pair of scissors for added dimension. Cut card windows, planters and a door from pink and cream card; ink around the edges of the windows and door to help them stand out. Fill the planters with punched flowers and add a punched flower smoke-trail from the chimney. Highlight the centre of the flowers with the flat back crystals.

CAREER LADDER

Congratulate high fliers on their latest promotion with this beautifully decorated card design. Tiny gold accent beads provide texture and colour in an instant; sprinkled over a ladder created from narrow double-sided tape, they stick like glue. The beaded ladder is trimmed with a selection of motifs that are easy to make yourself.

you will need

- **brown single fold card 21 x 10cm (8¼ x 4in)**
- **gold accent beads**
- **scraps of paper and card, small beads and wire for the decorations**

tip Make the rungs closer together at the top than at the bottom. Use a ruler to ensure that your lines are straight.

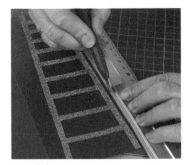

Step One Open out the brown single fold card and mark out a ladder in pencil on the front 5cm (2in) wide at the top and 7.5cm (3in) wide at the bottom. Place a strip of double-sided tape along each line. Don't overlap the tape – use a craft knife to trim any overlapping edges.

Step Two Peel-off the backing from the tape and tip the gold beads all over it. When all the tape is covered, collect the surplus beads and return them to the container. Use a paintbrush to wipe off any loose beads around the edges of the lines.

Step Three Cut along the right-hand edge of the ladder, leaving a narrow border of card.

Step Four Make a blue paper folder and wrap red wool or thread around the corners; stick in place using adhesive foam pads. Allow the folder to overlap the edge of the ladder, but make sure it does not protrude beyond the edge of the card back.

Step Five Fold a small piece of orange card in half and cut an aperture in the top front half; place a small piece of white paper inside and add a few scribbles to suggest writing. Secure in place.

Step Six Cut a bottle shape from green card and add gold paper around the neck and as a label. Thread gold beads onto wire; attach the wire to the back of the bottle. Stick bead 'bubbles' down the side of the card.

tip Small beads can roll a long way, so it is wise to work over a tray or piece of soft cloth to keep stray beads under control.

Lucky Four-Leaf Clover

Use a lino-cutting tool to carve a simple image into an ordinary stationery eraser and use it to stamp this good luck card (see Techniques: Stamping).

you will need

❀ green single fold card 16 x 9cm (6¼ x 3½in)
❀ white linen-effect and green card
❀ bottle green corrugated card
❀ homemade clover leaf stamp
❀ spring green and green Vivid Mini™ inkpads
❀ narrow yellow spotted sheer ribbon

Use your homemade stamp to stamp the four-leaf clover on the white card. Trim to 5 x 4cm (2 x 1½in) and mount on a slightly larger piece of green card. Trim the corrugated panel to make a tag and mount the leaf panel onto it; add the ribbon. Glue a strip of corrugated card to the bottom of the base card. Mount the tag with adhesive foam pads.

Good Luck

A ready-made stencil of the Chinese characters for 'lucky' has been used for this good luck card.

you will need

❀ red single fold card 17.5 x 8cm (7 x 3¼in)
❀ red card
❀ oriental character printed paper
❀ 'lucky' ready-made stencil
❀ gold embossing powder

Place the stencil over the red card, right side up, and use an embossing pen to colour in the characters. Remove the stencil, sprinkle the design with gold embossing powder, and heat emboss to produce a raised image (see Techniques: Heat Embossing). Trim the card so that it is just slightly wider than the motif, mount onto oriental character printed card, and then mount onto the red single fold card.

Lucky Black Cat

Make sure friends and family know that you are wishing them all the best in their endeavours with this lucky black cat card.

you will need

- silver single fold card 15 x 10cm (6 x 4in)
- red card
- black velvet paper
- cat punch

Punch three cats out of black velvet paper. Cut a panel of red card the same width as the single fold card and large enough to hold the punched cats. Stick the cats to the panel using a glue pen. Cut a panel of black velvet paper slightly wider than the red panel, and stick the red panel on top using double-sided tape. Stick to the front of the base card.

Happiness, Love and Prosperity

Bamboo is a Chinese symbol of good fortune while the stamped design spells outs a message of happiness, love and prosperity.

you will need

- dark green single fold card 15 x 10cm (6 x 4in)
- dark green, white and orange card
- bamboo-printed vellum
- happiness, love and prosperity rubber stamp
- VersaMark™ inkpad
- gold embossing powder
- seven orange eyelets
- thin dark green ribbon

Place a 14 x 9cm (5½ x 3½in) rectangle of bamboo-printed vellum over a piece of white card the same size and set orange eyelets in each corner to hold together. Cut a piece of orange card very slightly larger and stick the vellum panel on top; stick this panel to the front of the base card. Make a tag from orange and green card layers; heat emboss the Chinese message of good fortune to the centre of it. Place a vellum-covered card strip to the base and set the tag eyelets. Finally, tie a double length of narrow green ribbon through the top eyelet and attach the tag to the card using adhesive foam pads.

FOND FAREWELL

This concertina-style tag-shaped card is the perfect way to bid farewell to a colleague who is retiring as it has the maximum space for warm wishes from fellow workers. It is simple to cut and fold, and can be decorated on both the back and front to suit the hobbies and interests of the recipient.

you will need

- ⚙ **two sheets cream card A4 (US letter)**
- ⚙ **printed papers**
- ⚙ **green inkpad**
- ⚙ **photographs, ribbons, card scraps, buttons and other embellishments of your choice**

Step One To make a large tag template cut a 15 x 9cm (6 x 3½in) piece of scrap card. Measure and mark 2.5cm (1in) down from the top of each long edge and the same measurement across the top. Draw a line across each corner between the marks and cut along the lines.

Step Two Starting at one edge of the cream card, draw round the template to mark three tag shapes side by side and touching. Use the edge of the card as the side of the first tag. Cut out the three-tag shape.

Step Three Score and fold the lines where the tags meet, making the folds in opposite directions to create the concertina shape. Using the template again, draw the tag shape six times on the back of your chosen printed papers. Cut out each tag just inside the drawn lines.

Step Four Cut a 9 x 6cm (3½ x 2½in) rectangle from scrap card. Measure 2cm (¾in) in each direction from the top two corners as in Step 1, draw the diagonal lines and cut along them to create a tag shape. Use this template to cut five cream card tags.

Step Five Ink the edges of the cream card tags with the green inkpad. Stick the printed paper tags centrally onto each of the concertina pages – front and back – then centre a small cream tag on top and stick in place on all but the front page.

Step Six Decorate the card pages with photos of colleagues, trimmed and positioned on a card rectangle cut slightly larger. Stick in place at the top of the pages to leave plenty of space for greetings. Use buttons tied with thread bows to draw the eye.

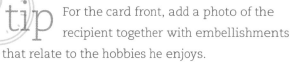

tip For the card front, add a photo of the recipient together with embellishments that relate to the hobbies he enjoys.

Vintage Celebration

Celebrate a retirement by cracking open a bottle of vintage wine, and let it inspire you to make this unusual retirement card.

you will need
- burgundy-coloured card A4 (US letter) sheet
- parchment paper
- black paper and gold pen

Using an embossing tool, emboss a grapes and leaves design onto parchment paper. Fold the burgundy-coloured card in half and cut into a wine bottle shape. Cut a rectangular aperture in the bottle shape and mount the embossed parchment paper behind it. Add a black paper stopper to the top of the bottle and embellish with the gold pen.

French Leave

This design is ideal for those who may be thinking of retiring abroad. Coloured pencils have been used to bring a real sense of depth to a stamped landscape.

you will need
- light brown folded card 15 x 10cm (6 x 4in)
- cream and dark brown card
- landscape with sunflowers rubber stamp
- coffee bean Brilliance™ inkpad
- colouring pencils
- tag punch
- four lilac eyelets
- raffia

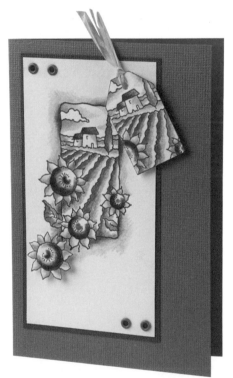

Stamp the landscape design three times onto cream card. Using colouring pencils, colour in two complete images and just the large sunflower head of the third. Trim down one image to 12.5 x 6.5cm (5 x 2½in). Punch a tag from the second image and cut out the sunflower head from the third. Punch a hole in the top of the tag; thread with raffia and tie in a knot. Mount the panel onto a slightly larger piece of dark brown card, then onto the base card to the left of centre. Set the eyelets. Mount the tag and sunflower head with adhesive foam pads.

tip Use soft-leaded colouring pencils for effective blending and a good pencil sharpener to maintain a sharp point.

Time to Fly

A pretty card, ideal for a woman's retirement, decorated with tag-shaped style stone embellishments.

you will need

- cream single fold card 14cm (5½in) square
- cream card
- collage and butterfly stamps
- mandarin and henna Ancient Page™ inkpads
- brown Crafter's™ inkpad
- two tag-shaped coated style stones
- copper leaf pen
- four copper snaps
- copper wire and beads

Sponge the style stones with mandarin and henna ink for a mottled effect; let dry, then stamp using the collage stamp; finally colour the edges with a copper leaf pen. Thread copper wire through the stamped tags, add a bead and curl the ends of the wire into a coil. Cut a piece of cream card 7.5 x 6.5cm (3 x 2½in), sponge, and then stamp. Use a piece of torn scrap paper to sponge a pale orange border along the sides of the base card. Use brown ink to stamp three butterflies down the right-hand side of the base card and colour in with a wet paintbrush. Fix the snaps to the stamped collage panel and mount; use adhesive dots to secure the tags to the card.

Good Luck on Your Retirement

The warm, rich colours of this card make it an ideal choice for a man on his retirement.

you will need

- cream single fold card 14.5cm (5¾in) square
- cream and burgundy card
- large leaf stamp
- black inkpad
- bleach
- two small burgundy leaf buttons
- narrow wired ribbon

Stamp the large leaf design twice on burgundy card and use a paintbrush dipped into a few drops of bleach to bleach out the colour. One bleached panel becomes the base panel, while the other provides leaves for cutting out. Attach the cut out leaves with adhesive foam pads. Layer onto the single fold card first a burgundy card square, then a cream card rectangle, and finally the central stamped panel. Securely fix the buttons for an extra decorative element.

FIRST DAY

Starting school is an important milestone that calls for a special card such as this. It is created by filling a sheet of transparent pockets, usually used for photographic slides, with stickers, embellishments, photos and other precious items. The child who receives the pocket card can keep adding to it, for example when they receive a star or sticker for good work at school, or with photos of classmates.

you will need

- ☆ white single fold card 18cm (7in) square
- ☆ paper in a selection of colours
- ☆ clear 35mm slide pockets
- ☆ aqua self-adhesive foam 18cm (7in) square
- ☆ little boy and pencil rubber stamps
- ☆ red and blue inkpads
- ☆ wavy-edge scissors
- ☆ embellishments – photographs; plastic and card frames; number and letter dots and stickers; pencil case charms; brightly coloured paper fasteners; school photo stickers

Step One Cut out a square of nine pockets from the slide sheet. Trim away the excess plastic as close as possible to the seams for a neat finish. Measure and cut out nine 5cm (2in) squares of coloured paper to fit inside the pockets. Decorate following the examples in Steps 2–5.

Step Two Apply a 'tick' sticker in the middle of a blue paper square, then stamp a little boy with red ink in each corner. Stamp pencils down each side of a light blue square using blue ink. Add a crayons photo sticker in the centre. Punch a small hole in each corner of the sticker and insert a paper fastener in each.

Step Three Attach a school bag photo sticker to a yellow paper square, positioning it off-centre. Trim another crayon sticker to leave only the pencil tops showing and stick it vertically down the side of the paper.

Step Four Stick a selection of framed and unframed number stickers to a lime green paper square. Decorate an orange paper square with alphabet stickers. Attach three pencil case charms to a blue paper square before trimming the edges with wavy-edge scissors and sticking to another orange square.

Step Five Make a drawing and lettering in the style of a child on white paper and attach to a green paper square. Push out the centre of the card frame. Glue the photo of the child who is starting school to the back, then attach it to a red paper square.

Step Six Stick the aqua foam sheet to the front of the white card. Insert each decorated square carefully into a slide pocket, positioning the photo square in the centre. Attach a small piece of double-sided tape to the back of each pocket, and mount onto the foam-covered card, pressing firmly in place.

☆ **tip** To make the child's writing and drawing look as authentic as possible, do it with your left hand (or vice versa if you're left-handed).

Winner's Trophy

Celebrate sporting successes with this trophy card, which could be personalized with rubdown letters.

you will need

- ☆ silver single fold card 21 x 14.8cm (8¼ x 5⅞in)
- ☆ thin silver mirror and gold card
- ☆ thick green and printed papers
- ☆ three small blue tags
- ☆ silver football peel-off stickers
- ☆ silver snap fasteners
- ☆ very narrow light aqua satin ribbon

Glue a green 21 x 9cm (8¼ x 3½in) paper strip to the right-hand side of the base card. Cut a silver mirror card trophy (see Templates). Cut the shield from gold card, decorate with a football peel-off sticker and attach to the trophy with silver snap fasteners. Cut three small squares from printed papers and glue to the left-hand side of the base card to make the pockets for the tags. Decorate the tags with the peel-off stickers, and pop one in each pocket. Finally, fix the trophy in place with adhesive foam pads.

tip Use a craft knife to cut out small fiddly, enclosed areas.

Gymkhana Success

A large rosette provides the central image on this card to celebrate success at the gymkhana.

you will need

- ☆ white single fold card 21 x 14.8cm (8¼ x 5⅞in)
- ☆ spotted and checked scrapbooking papers
- ☆ sporting and horse sticker
- ☆ tag punch
- ☆ narrow gingham ribbon

Cover the front of the single fold card with spotted paper. Cut a 21 x 4cm (8¼ x 1½in) strip from checked paper. Cut three slots on the strip large enough to slip in the tags. Punch out three tags, decorate each with a sticker and finish off with a ribbon. Decorate the front of the card with a paper rosette and stick a horse sticker to its centre.

An Apple for Teacher

At the end of the school year a thank you card for teacher is a lovely idea. For more on using punches see Techniques: Punching.

you will need

☆ stone single fold card 13cm (5in) square

☆ light and dark green paper

☆ apple and square punch

Punch a row of three apple shapes from the light green paper, leaving a space of 4cm (1½in) between each apple. Repeat with the dark green paper. Place the square punch upside down and slide the punched light green paper into the square punch so that a punched-out apple is positioned centrally in the square. Press down firmly. Repeat with the remaining punched-out apples. Glue the punched-out apple squares onto the single fold card, alternating the colours. Glue the apples inside the punched-out apple shapes, again alternating the two shades to create a contrast.

tip This card can be made in minutes – use a heart for Valentines or a Mother's Day flower.

Music Exams

This card is ideal for celebrating music exam success – just change the musical instrument to match your child's interest.

you will need

☆ white single fold card 14 x 8.5cm (5½ x 3¼in)

☆ musical score, musical collage and treble clef stamp

☆ VersaMark™ inkpad

☆ Funstamps Verdi Gris embossing powder

☆ clear embossing powder

☆ yellow and blue watercolour paints

Stamp the front of the single fold card with the musical score and heat emboss with the Verdi Gris embossing powder. Stamp the collage image onto four pieces of white card. Heat emboss three pieces using clear embossing powder and one using the Verdi Gris. Brush with the watercolour paints and allow the colours to mingle together softly. Once dry, cut each layer progressively smaller. Use adhesive foam pads to stick the layers together, and secure to the front of the card. Stamp and heat emboss the treble clef on a small scrap of white card and fix in place.

THE GRADUATE

This congratulatory design is suitably distinguished to commemorate the academic achievement of a university graduate, featuring a replica of the formal headgear worn for the occasion – the distinctively shaped mortarboard – complete with a handmade tassel. A ribbon-tied scrolled certificate provides an additional ceremonious note.

you will need

☆ burgundy horizontal
single fold card
15 x 21cm (6 x 8¼in)

☆ script printed and sand-
coloured paper

☆ black craft foam

☆ black embroidery thread

☆ narrow red satin ribbon

tip Use scissors to trim the ends of the ribbon in a 'V' shape.

Step One Using the mortarboard template (see Templates), draw around it onto the black craft foam with a white pencil and cut out.

Step Two Cut a 15cm (6in) length of black embroidery thread. Cut a piece of scrap card 6 x 15cm (2⅜ x 6in). Place the thread across the top of the card and secure with masking tape. Cut a 2.5m (2¾yd) length of thread and wind it around the middle of the card.

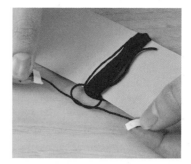

Step Three Remove the taped thread ends from the card and tie tightly in a knot around all the loops of thread wound around the card. Tie a second tight knot to make the first secure. Slide the card out.

Step Four Cut another 15cm (6in) length of thread and place it under the threads 1cm (⅜in) down from the knot just made. Take either end of this piece of thread and tie a double knot around all the threads. Leave the ends to hang down.

Step Five Cut through the looped threads at the opposite end to those tied. Trim the thread ends so that they all hang level. Attach the tassel to the foam hat with adhesive tape.

Step Six Tear two rectangles of script paper, one about 14 x 20cm (5½ x 8in) and another 8 x 18cm (3¼ x 7in). Glue the larger to the base card right side up; glue the smaller right side down on top of the first at an angle. Glue the mortarboard on. Roll up a piece of sand-coloured paper; tie the red ribbon in a double knot around the middle, and attach using double-sided tape.

tip Instead of using script paper, you could personalize the background by scanning and printing the exam certificate.

Well Done

Many exams have to be passed before graduating, and this design is ideal for celebrating success along the way.

you will need
- ☆ bronze single fold card 17.5 x 8cm (7 x 3¼in)
- ☆ silver card
- ☆ script paper
- ☆ star punch
- ☆ silver craft wire

Stick two hand-torn strips of script paper to the top and bottom of the base card. Make a tiny envelope from white paper (see Techniques: Making Envelopes), slip a tiny piece of folded script paper inside and glue onto the card. Coil three lengths of silver wire and attach punched silver stars to one end with double-sided adhesive tape; glue in place.

tip   A special message of congratulations could be attached to one of the wire coils.

Quick Graduation

Stickers are used to make this simple yet stylish graduation card.

you will need
- ☆ opal single fold card 15 x 10cm (6 x 4in)
- ☆ blue and gold card
- ☆ mortarboard and scroll sticker
- ☆ star punch

Cut a square of blue card a little wider than the mortarboard and stick in place. Mount onto gold card with double-sided tape and trim, leaving a narrow border. Stick in the centre top of the base card. Cut a strip of blue card the width of the base card, and add the scroll and two punched out gold stars. Mount this panel onto gold card, leaving a narrow border showing at the top and bottom, and stick to the lower section of the base card.

Driving Test Success

These funky little cars make for a fun card to celebrate a driving test pass.

you will need
☆ black single fold card 21 x 10cm (8¼ x 4in)
☆ printed, black and pink paper
☆ eight coloured buttons
☆ white thread

Tie white thread through each button. Cut four cars from printed papers (see Templates). Stick the cars on black paper and trim around each one, leaving a very narrow black outline. Stick the cars down the middle of a pink paper rectangle and stick on the wheels. Glue to the front of the single fold card.

life's special moments ☆ more for EXAM SUCCESS

New Driver

Use a page from an old road atlas to create the background panel for this congratulations card.

you will need
☆ red single fold card 15cm (6in) square
☆ white, red and silver card
☆ road atlas page
☆ car rubber stamp
☆ black inkpad
☆ key punch

Cover the front of the red single fold card with a road atlas panel. Stamp the car image onto white card, cut out and colour in. Punch a circle from red card and thread on punched silver keys to make a key fob. Make an 'L' plate from red and white card and tear it in half. Use adhesive foam pads to stick the decorations onto the card.

tip You can add shine to the car windscreen and headlights using a dimensional liquid.

BON VOYAGE

A collage of stamped images is combined on this stylish card to wish a traveller bon voyage on a special holiday trip. A colour-wash technique is worked with a paintbrush across the stamped images to unify the design, and the overall effect achieved is of a vintage travelogue. Colour washing is an easy, effective way of filling open areas of the design.

TRAVEL

life's special moments

you will need

- cream linen-effect single fold card 12cm (4¾in) square
- cream linen-effect card
- light pink vellum

- French woman, 'bon voyage' background, manuscript background and 'par avion' and cancellation postmark stamps

- fuchsia, purple and orange Vivid™ inkpads
- graphite black Brilliance™ inkpad
- black permanent pen

- tag punch
- three lilac eyelets
- white string
- one large and one small pink button

Step One Using the fuchsia inkpad, stamp the French woman on a piece of cream linen-effect card. Using a wet paintbrush, drag out the colour from the stamped lines to fill some of the background areas and even out the colour in the solid stamped areas where you can see the grain of the linen-effect card. Once dry, trim the card around the border of the image.

Step Two Using the purple inkpad, stamp the 'bon voyage' background on another piece of cream linen-effect card. Colour wash (see Step 1) just over the 'bon voyage'. Once completely dry, highlight with a fine-tip pen (you can use a heat gun to speed up the drying process).

Step Three Turn the tag punch upside down. Slip the bon voyage-stamped card into the punch. Move it around until the words 'bon voyage' are positioned within the opening; punch out. Make a hole in the top of the tag.

Step Four Place the stamped panel and tag on a piece of scrap paper. Pick up some ink from the orange inkpad and gently sponge over both items. Keep to the edges on the tag, but apply colour over the open areas of the picture. Once dry, fix an eyelet in the tag hole, thread the string through and tie in a knot.

Step Five Using the black inkpad, stamp the manuscript background onto the vellum. Allow to dry before tearing away the edges. Arrange all the items, including the buttons, on the base card. Once you have decided on the arrangement, remove and stamp the 'par avion' and postmarks in a gap using the fuchsia and black inkpads.

Step Six Secure the vellum to the single fold card using an eyelet in each of two opposite corners. Using spray glue, mount the stamped panel onto the vellum, fix the tag in place with adhesive foam pads and the buttons with PVA (white) glue.

tip Perfect your colour-wash technique. Too much painting and the stamped images can disappear; too little and the washes look patchy.

Holiday of a Lifetime

This card is perfect for friends or family who are going on that once-in-a-lifetime holiday or moving overseas.

you will need

- copper single fold card 12cm (4¾in) square
- copper card
- antique map paper
- antique travel tag stickers
- string

Cut a square of antique map paper slightly smaller than the copper single fold card and stick it to the front with double-sided tape, leaving a border all around. Stick the tag stickers to copper card and cut out leaving a border of copper showing. Punch holes in the tags then thread them onto string; wrap the string all the way around the front of the card and knot above the top tag. Secure the tags in place using adhesive foam pads, positioned each side of the string.

Travel Memories

A card with a pocket for storing mementoes of a trip, such as tickets, postcards or photographs.

you will need

- white card 21 x 29.5cm (8¼ x 11⅝in) plus small pieces for stamping
- printed papers including a handwritten script design
- travel rubber stamps
- chestnut and sienna chalk inkpads
- lemon and blue chalk
- narrow brown satin ribbon

Fold the piece of white card 7cm (2¾in) from the left and right edge, to make a zigzag. Cover the front panel with a cream printed paper, and the inside with the handwritten script. Cut an 8 x 15cm (3⅛ x 5⅞in) strip from diamond printed paper and glue to the inside of the card to make a pocket. Stamp travel images onto white card and apply chalks to add colour. Glue to the inside of the card, tucking them into the pocket slightly.

tip To finish, thread the ribbon through an embellished card buckle and glue onto the pocket.

Pack Your Bags

Wish the whole family all the best for their holiday with this simple-to-make card.

you will need

- cream single fold card 21.5 x 11.5cm (8½ x 4¼in)
- light brown, dark brown and cream paper
- aeroplane, train and car rubber stamps
- blue inkpad
- string

Stamp around the edges of the single fold card with the vehicle stamps; once dry, colour in with colouring pencils. For the suitcases, cut three rectangles of dark brown paper descending in size; cut and glue on suitcase corners and handles made from the light brown paper, adding felt-tip pen detailing. Attach tiny cream luggage labels, tied with string. Mount the suitcases onto the card using adhesive foam pads.

you will need

- black single fold card 10 x 14.5cm (4 x 5¾in)
- glossy paper
- black, peach, white, lime green and yellow card
- large solid circle and tropical landscape rubber stamps
- VersaMark™ inkpad
- desert heat Kaleidacolor™ inkpad
- graphite black Brilliance™ inkpad
- die-cutting tool and large and small Hawaiian flowers and sailing boat dies
- brayer
- deckle-edged scissors

Honeymoon Cruise

This design featuring a setting sun on a holiday 'photo' is the perfect 'bon voyage' card for a honeymooning couple.

Using the VersaMark™ inkpad, stamp a circle in the centre of the glossy paper. Ink up the brayer with the Kaleidacolor™ inkpad and roll over the paper several times. Once dry stamp the landscape across the sunset with black ink. Trim the paper to 4.5 x 7cm (1¾ x 2¾in). Mount on black card and trim the edges with deckle-edged scissors. Using the Kaleidacolor™ inkpad, stamp the landscape across the bottom of a piece of peach card cut slightly smaller than the base card. Die-cut and assemble a large Hawaiian flower; also a few small flowers. Mount the sunset panel with adhesive foam pads. Glue the flowers around the photo. Die-cut a sailing boat and mount with adhesive foam pads.

KEY BIRTHDAY

A 21st birthday is a landmark occasion and deserves a special card to celebrate. This design is so quick and easy to make but looks sensational. The number 21 and the keys spell out the occasion. The punched key has also been used as a stencil to decorate the base card. The metallic thread and beads and crystal-embellished daisy chain peel-off sticker make for a luxurious look.

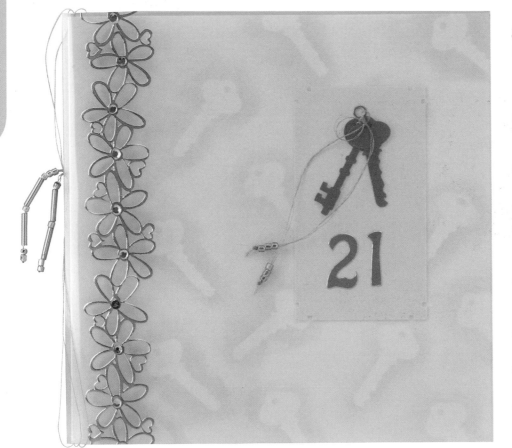

you will need

- ✳ white with gold sparkle single fold card 14.8cm (5¾in) square
- ✳ clear single fold card 14.8cm (5¾in) square
- ✳ soft green and gold card
- ✳ pale green inkpad
- ✳ square corner cutter and keys punches
- ✳ eyelet, numbers and daisy chain peel-off stickers
- ✳ gold metallic thread
- ✳ seed and bugle beads
- ✳ flat back crystals

Step One Cut a piece of soft green card 8 x 4.5cm (3⅛ x 1¾in) and punch the corners using the square corner cutter. Punch keys from the gold card. Use a hole punch to make two holes, one above the other, in the centre top; stick peel-off eyelets over the holes. Thread through metallic thread, and decorate at either end with a few seed beads.

Step Two Thread on the keys, and tie the thread in a bow. Take the numbers 2 and 1 from the sticker sheet, and position under the keys. Use a craft knife to help you place them accurately.

Step Three Using one of the punched keys as a stencil, gently sponge green ink around the key on the front of the base card. Stencil the key motifs randomly all over, making sure they tip over the edge of the card to give a more professional finish.

Step Four Position the strip of green card centrally and slightly towards the top of the single fold card. Stick in place with double-sided tape.

Step Five Position the daisy chain peel-off sticker down the folded edge on the front of the clear card and trim off any excess. Add flat back crystals to highlight the centres of the daisies using dimensional glue.

Step Six Cut a length of metallic thread approximately three times the length of the card. Thread the bugle and seed beads onto the thread, and tie knots at both ends. Place the white and gold card inside the clear card and use the thread to tie the two cards together at the fold (allow the knot to fall about a third of the way down the folded edge of the card).

Happy 18th

Combine simple stamping with large number stickers for a stunning 18th birthday celebration card.

you will need

- silver linen-effect single fold card 13.5cm (5¼in) square
- mid-blue, light blue and silver linen-effect card
- Mediterranean blue and starlite black Brilliance™ inkpads
- die-cutting tool and two different number fonts, tag and star dies
- thin blue ribbon

Use die-cut foam numbers to stamp an all-over background design of 18s on a 10cm (4in) square of mid-blue card. First stamp the numbers with blue ink, let dry, and then stamp the black ones in between and overlapping. Mount onto a slightly larger piece of light blue card, then onto a slightly larger mid-blue card square and then onto the single fold card. Thread a die-cut tag with ribbon and decorate with a die-cut star. Mount the tag, die-cut outline star and numbers on the card, using adhesive foam pads for the tag.

Flower Power 18th

This super see-through card is decorated with flowers die-cut from brightly coloured pearlescent card.

Cut the acetate card in half. Cut a 15 x 10cm (6 x 4in) strip of pink textured card; score to make a concertina-fold spine; attach to the acetate with double-sided tape and cover with pink card strips on the inside. Die-cut different-sized flowers from pearlescent card; punch circles to stick to the flower centres, mixing and matching colours. Overlap petals to glue together and fix to the mountain fold inside the card. On the card front, stick a solid and outline flower so that the acetate is sandwiched in between; decorate with a die-cut 18. Add glitter highlights. Thread ribbons through evenly-spaced double holes punched in the front spine.

you will need

- acetate single fold card 15cm (6in) square
- pink textured card
- pink, orange and cherry pearlescent card
- die-cutting tool and flower and number dies
- small, medium and large circle punches
- glitter glue and assorted narrow ribbons

Starburst 18

This large number card would make a wonderful party invitation.

you will need
- blue single fold card 21 x 15cm (8¼ x 5⅞in)
- starburst rubber stamp
- blue inkpad
- 18 confetti

Trace off the 18 template (see Templates), transfer to the front of the card and cut out. Randomly stamp blue starbursts all over and stick the confetti to the starburst centres using a glue pen.

tip Make your own card blank from an A4 (US letter) sheet of card halved, then scored and folded to make A5.

Starburst 21

There will be no mistaking what is being celebrated with this shaped card.

you will need
- blackcurrant single fold card 21 x 15cm (8¼ x 5⅞in)
- starburst rubber stamp
- white inkpad
- 21 confetti

Trace off the 21 template (see Templates), transfer to the front of the card and cut out. Randomly stamp white starbursts over; stick the confetti to the centre of the starburst centres using a glue pen.

tip These shaped cards are great for boys and girls – simply change the colour to fit.

Birthdays

What better reason to make a card than to celebrate the birthday of family and friends, from sons and daughters to husbands and wives, from baby's first to a best friend's 40th, there is the perfect design just waiting to be made.

Choose from a pop-up teddy or a cute folding chick to delight the toddlers, or a flip-up phone and BMX biker's carousel for older boys and girls. Teenage girls will adore the fashion charm card, and the action-packed soccer card will appeal to teenage guys.

For men, there's a gold-embossed dreamboat for keen sailors, and for women who love to shop, a beautiful iris-folded purse, while bright balloons and beautifully gift-wrapped presents are great motifs for anyone celebrating a birthday.

MY FIRST YEAR

This concertina keepsake card makes an ideal 1st birthday card. It is designed as a mini album of mementoes and photographs to provide a delightful record of a little girl's first year of life. The main focus of the card is baby's photograph, displayed on an embellished tag, and inside is a fold-out collection of precious memories, in this case a little sock and a lock of hair.

birthdays | LITTLE GIRL

you will need

- white single fold card 14 x 8.8cm (5½ x 3½in)
- cream paper
- pink gingham paper
- luggage label
- baby photos and mementoes
- paper ribbon sticker
- five daisy stickers
- heart-shaped button
- pink twine
- self-adhesive ribbon
- wavy-edge and zigzag-edge scissors

Step One Apply glue to the card front and line up one straight edge of a 17.5 x 14cm (5½ x 7in) piece of gingham paper with the card edge and press in place. Fold the excess to the back before gluing in place. Use wavy-edge scissors to cut narrow borders from cream paper and glue to the top and bottom of the card.

Step Two Using zigzag-edge scissors, cut a piece of cream paper the same width as the luggage label and 4cm (1½in) shorter; glue in the centre of the label. Attach the paper ribbon sticker to the lower edge and trim to fit. Cut a wavy gingham border for the top of the ribbon sticker and a wavy cream border for the bottom, and glue in place.

Step Three Cut a 4.5cm (1¾in) square from gingham paper. Draw a smaller square in the centre and carefully cut out to make a frame; glue to the label. Wrap pink twine around below the frame and tie the ends together on the back to keep it in place. Remove the label string and stick a daisy sticker over the hole; punch a hole in the sticker and tie a length of pink twine through it.

Step Four Glue the baby photo to thin card and trim it to fit inside the frame. Attach with adhesive foam pads. Glue the label to white card and trim the edges with wavy-edge scissors; mount onto the card front and stick on the heart button. Attach daisy stickers below the label. Arrange the ends of the pink twine and secure them with another daisy sticker in the top left-hand corner.

Step Five To make the concertina, cut three 15.5 x 22cm (6 x 8¾in) pieces of cream paper. Glue them together, overlapping the edges by 1.3cm (½in). Once dry, fold into five equal sections.

Step Six Glue a small memento, photo or sticker to each page of the concertina and decorate with borders of self-adhesive ribbon. Stick the concertina to the inside of the card and fold up the pages.

tip Mount small or fiddly items, such as a lock of hair, onto a small tag or swing ticket first for a neater appearance.

Baby Bear

A bright and cheerful stamped bear design ready with a hug for a toddler's birthday.

you will need
- purple single fold card 12.5cm (5in) square
- glossy card
- yellow card
- small and large bear rubber stamps
- VersaMark™ inkpad
- black Brilliance™ inkpad
- pastel colour inks and brayer
- flower punch

Stamp the small bear design over a square panel cut from the glossy card using the VersaMark™ inkpad; once dry, brayer with pastel-coloured inks. Mount onto a slightly larger yellow card panel, then mount onto the front of the single fold card. Stamp the large bear with the black Brilliance™ inkpad on a piece of brayered card. Use any leftover brayered card to punch out flowers. Mount the bear and flowers onto the card with adhesive foam pads.

you will need
- yellow card 12 x 30cm (4¾ x 12in)
- green, pink, white and orange paper
- daisy punch
- zigzag-edge scissors

Sweet Folding Chicks

Little children will enjoy the element of surprise with this folding card.

Divide the yellow card into four equal sections and concertina fold. Transfer the chick template (see Templates) to the top fold of the concertina. Hold all the sections of the card firmly together and cut out taking care that the chicks, once opened, will still be joined at the beak and tummy. Cut a strip of green paper with zigzag scissors and glue along the bottom. Punch daisies from white paper and glue onto the green strip. Use a small hole punch to cut the flower centres from pink paper. Cut the chicks' beaks and wings from orange paper and stick on. Use a black pen to mark the eyes.

One Today

A single candle cut from printed paper and layered onto pink card panels is an ideal decoration for baby's first birthday.

you will need

- pink single fold card 21 x 10 cm (8¼ x 4in)
- pink tag
- pink printed paper and card
- glitter glue
- very narrow pink gingham ribbon

Make a candle decoration: cut from printed paper and layer onto two pink card panels cut out to the candle's shape, but leaving a narrow border. Stick ribbon around the bottom half of the tag and stick the candle on top using adhesive foam pads. Add glitter glue to highlight the candle. Stick a strip of patterned pink paper to the single fold card with double-sided tape and attach the tag on top using adhesive foam pads.

Toddler's Gift

Turn a square single fold card into a gift box shape. Choose a bright colour, decorate with an animal stamp, and you have the perfect card for little ones.

you will need

- orange single fold card 16 x 14cm (6¼ x 5½in)
- lime green, yellow, orange and fuchsia card
- lion rubber stamp
- graphite black Brilliance™ inkpad
- 2.5cm (1in) circle punch

Work with the fold of the card at the top, and trim off the sides of the card at an angle, from 3cm (1¹/₈in) in from each side to the base corners, to give the present shape. Stamp the lion at random all over the card front. Make the 'ribbon' from yellow and lime card and glue card 'confetti' in between the lions. Stamp a single lion on lime green, yellow and orange card. Leave to dry. Cut out the lion from the yellow card, leaving a narrow border; cut out the head and mane from the green card; and the head only from the orange card. Assemble and stick to the ribbon crossover. Add a number sticker if desired.

FIRST BIRTHDAY SURPRISE

All babies love the game of peek-a-boo, and this surprising card is bound to delight a little boy on his 1st birthday. The 'lid' is stuck to the top of teddy's head; when it is lifted, the teddy's friendly face pops up out of the card pocket, while a cleverly constructed card 'stopper' prevents it from being pulled out completely.

you will need

- mustard single fold card 15 x 13cm (6 x 5⅛in)
- mustard card pieces – 15 x 10cm (6 x 4in) rectangle; 15 x 4cm (6 x 1½in) strip; 15cm (6in) square
- printed paper – 15 x 10cm (6 x 4in) rectangle; 15 x 4cm (6 x 1½in) strip; 14 x 2.5cm (5½ x 1in) strip
- teddy bear face
- wide blue satin ribbon

tip This card opens just like any other – but if you lift the lid there's a surprise in store.

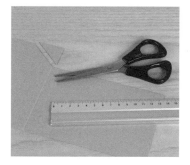

Step One
Measure 3cm (1³⁄₁₆in) down the back of the mustard single fold card and draw a guideline across the back and cut away. Along the top of the front measure 3.5cm (1³⁄₈in) from the fold. Draw a guideline from this point to the fold and carefully cut off this triangle.

Step Two
Flip the triangle over and place over the other top back corner. Lay your ruler against it, remove the triangle and draw in a guideline on the card back. Cut off this triangle too. Set the adapted single fold card aside.

Step Three
Glue the printed paper rectangle onto the mustard card rectangle. Turn over and, keeping as near to the edge as possible, apply 5mm (³⁄₁₆in) double-sided tape along the bottom and up both sides. Measure 2cm (¾in) in from each top corner and apply double-sided tape here too. Add a 1.5cm (⅝in) piece centrally at the bottom.

Step Four
Glue the bear centrally onto the mustard card square. To make a stopper: find the centre bottom of the face and measure 6.5cm (2⁹⁄₁₆in) out to each side; measure 1cm (³⁄₈in) above and below this line. Cut around the bear's face and stopper. Check that it fits between the tape on the mustard rectangle, and that the gap between the tape at the top is wide enough for the face to pass through but not the stopper.

Step Five
Remove the backing paper from the tape along the bottom of the rectangle. Cut 20cm (8in) of ribbon and wrap it centrally around the rectangle, keeping the join on the inside and at the bottom. Lay the bear and stopper on the single fold card, removing the remaining backing paper from the tape to secure the rectangle on top, trapping the bear and stopper inside.

Step Six
Create the box lid by gluing the wider printed paper strip onto the card strip. Turn over and measure 1cm (³⁄₈in) up from the bottom and draw a guideline. Wrap ribbon around the lid and tie in a bow. Lay the box lid on top of the face to decide where to secure it. Holding both layers in place, turn the face and lid over. Apply glue above the guideline to stick the face to the lid. (Not gluing below the line enables the box lid to overlap the box, giving a realistic appearance.) Neaten by gluing the thin strip of paper over the join.

Rocket Boy

This cosmic card is made from shiny holographic paper and the addition of star stickers gives the effect of a twinkling night sky.

Cover the front card with blue holographic paper. Construct the rocket from a white card base decorated with coloured holographic paper or, alternatively, use a rocket sticker. Glue a card bar vertically to the lower fin and attach to the centre of the card with a paper fastener. Loosely fold back the legs of the fastener on the reverse to allow the rocket to rotate freely across the top of the card. Cut a round moon from holographic paper to hide the bar and fastener. Decorate with star stickers and 'planets' made from circles punched from silver and gold paper.

you will need

- white single fold card 15cm (6in) square
- holographic paper in a variety of colours
- star stickers
- paper fastener

tip Cover the legs of the paper fastener on the inside of the card with a small square of paper to keep little fingers safe.

Three Today

Transform the number 3 into a train track to delight a little boy on his birthday.

you will need

- blue single fold card 20 x 15cm (8 x 6in)
- navy blue, red and brown card
- train stickers
- silver glitter glue
- zigzag-edge scissors

Cut a large number 3 from navy blue card and add sleepers cut from thin brown card edged with glitter glue for the rails. Mount the number with adhesive foam pads and apply train stickers around the edge. Cut a strip of red card with zigzag-edge scissors and glue to the folded edge.

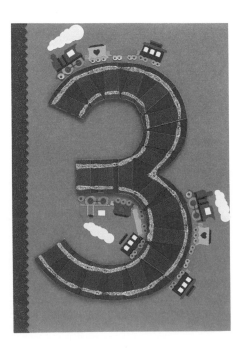

A Trip to the Zoo

One large stamp featuring several different animals is used here. The stamped design is cut up and rearranged to create a bold collage.

you will need

- blue single fold card 14cm (5½in) square
- white, blue and green card
- blue and green striped paper
- animal rubber stamp
- Mediterranean blue Brilliance™ inkpad
- die-cutting tool and number die
- four blue brads
- green and white spotted button
- very narrow blue sheer ribbon

Stamp the animal design twice onto white card; cut out two elephants, two fish, one lion and one giraffe and decorate with washes of green and blue felt-tip. Glue a panel of striped paper to the front of the card. Die-cut the number appropriate to the child's age from green card, mount on a small blue card square and fix a brad in each corner. Thread a short length of the ribbon through the holes of the button and tie in a double knot. Arrange and mount the animal and number panels and button onto the base card, raising some of the panels with adhesive foam pads.

....

Animals in the Box

Spring into action and coil wire to add bobbing 3D animal decorations to this fun birthday card.

you will need

- purple single fold card 21 x 10cm (8¼ x 4in)
- grey, pink, orange, white, brown and yellow card
- yellow plain and printed paper
- 24-gauge silver wire
- star punch
- narrow yellow ribbon

Make three wire coils from 30cm (12in) lengths of silver wire (see Techniques: Metal and Wire). Make three animal heads (make from circles of paper or card, or use stickers, punched shapes or die-cuts instead). Attach a wire coil to the back of each head. Make a parcel from yellow card covered with printed paper; cut and attach two box flaps from yellow paper. Add a ribbon tie. Use tape to attach the wire coils to the back flap so that the spring comes forward in front of the parcel. Decorate the card background with punched stars and mount the parcel with adhesive foam pads.

KITTY CAT BIRTHDAY

This pretty, pink kitty cat card will delight young girls who will love the cute kitten buttons which have been made from shrink plastic. The cats are stamped, cut out and heated up. They shrink before your very eyes to about 40 per cent of their original size so remember to punch the buttonholes before you heat them.

you will need

- 🐱 light pink single fold card 15 x 10cm (6 x 4in)
- 🐱 bright pink card A4 (US letter) sheet
- 🐱 sheet of shrink plastic
- 🐱 sanding block
- 🐱 cat rubber stamp
- 🐱 black permanent inkpad
- 🐱 pink embroidery and wispy silver thread
- 🐱 pink gel pen

Step One Sand the sheet of shrink plastic using the sanding block. Rub in all directions to take the glossy finish off. Wipe off the dust. Stamp out four cat designs onto the sheet leaving plenty of room between them. Leave to dry for a few minutes.

Step Two Cut out the cats, leaving a slight border around them. Use a 3mm (⅛in) hole punch to create two holes for the buttons.

Step Three Working on a heat-resistant board, and holding each cat in place with a craft knife, apply heat with a heat gun. The shrink plastic will twist and curl as it shrinks. Keep applying heat to the cat until it finally flattens out. Take the edge of the rubber stamp and press it down on top of the cat to make sure it is nice and flat.

Step Four Cut short lengths of pink embroidery thread. Thread through the buttonholes to the front and tie in a knot. Use the gel pen to colour the flowers around the cats' necks and leave to dry.

Step Five Place the light pink single fold card on a piece of scrap card and randomly stamp cats all over the front. Make sure some of the cats spill over the edges to give a professional finish. Leave to dry, then colour in all the flowers around the cats' necks with the pink gel pen.

Step Six Stamp two cat designs onto the bright pink card, with space between them. Leave to dry then cut around them to make two oblongs and fix to the left-hand side of the card front with adhesive foam pads. Cut a strip of bright pink card 11 x 2cm (4½ x ⅝in) and cut off the top corners to make a long tag. Stick the evenly positioned cat buttons to the tag with double-sided tape. Punch a hole in the top of the tag and loop the silver thread through. Secure to the right with adhesive foam pads.

tip Choose simple, bold designs to make buttons out of shrink plastic; intricate motifs may tear as you cut them.

Party Dress

A very pretty stamped party dress has been dry embossed onto vellum to give a frosted appearance, and seed beads and flower eyelet peel-off stickers add the finishing touches.

you will need

- orange single fold pearlescent card 16 x 11.5cm (6¼ x 4½in)
- white card
- white crystal vellum A4 (US letter) sheet
- dress rubber stamp
- pearlescent orange Brilliance™ inkpad
- white flower eyelet peel-off stickers
- orange seed beads

Stamp three dresses on vellum. Once dry, trim a rectangle around one, which becomes the base dress; dry emboss the bodice (see Techniques: Dry Embossing). On the second dress dry emboss just the skirt, and on the third, just the two outer sections of the skirt; cut out. Starting with the larger piece, stick the skirt layers onto the base dress using dots of PVA (white) glue along the back edges of each. Sponge the edges of the vellum with orange ink. Mount the dress panel onto a slightly larger piece of white card. Punch a hole in each corner and decorate with the flower eyelets. Mount the panel centrally and stick orange seed beads over the dots on the dress using PVA (white) glue.

Quick Present Card

Resin peel-off stickers are an absolute essential for the last-minute cardmaker's emergency supplies.

you will need

- pink single fold card 12.5cm (5in) square
- orange card
- present resin peel-off stickers

Cut a panel of orange card about 1.3cm (½in) smaller all round than the single fold card and glue on centrally. Now fill the orange panel with different-shaped present stickers.

Flip-Up Phone

Young girls will love the happy face flip-up mobile (cell) phone that decorates this birthday card design.

you will need

- white single fold card 18cm (7in) square
- black and silver card
- striped scrapbooking paper
- holographic paper
- girl rubber stamp
- brown inkpad
- 3D smiley stickers

Cut the open phone from silver card (see Templates); fold in half so that the silver side is inside. Use a white card square decorated with a coloured in stamped design to decorate the top half, and the 3D smiley stickers to create a keypad on the bottom half. Close and mount in the centre of the single fold card, which has been covered with striped paper. Cut the closed phone from holographic paper and stick to the front of the closed phone. Add the phone detailing using the black and silver card, and add a smiley sticker to finish.

Dancing Girls

This would make a great invitation to a girl's birthday party. A dancing girl stamp is repeated across the card with a pretty pink-fringed flower border above and below.

you will need

- pink single fold card 15 x 10cm (6 x 4in)
- pale yellow card
- dancing girl rubber stamp
- VersaMark™ inkpad
- silver embossing powder
- light and dark pink 1cm (³/₈in) wide quilling paper strips
- orange 3mm (¹/₈in) wide quilling paper strips
- fringing and quilling tool

Make twelve fringed and coiled flowers, six from light and six from dark pink paper (see Techniques: Quilling). Stamp the dancing girl design three times across a rectangle of the pale yellow card and heat emboss with silver powder (see Techniques: Heat Embossing). Once dry, colour in with felt-tip pens. Mount the stamped panel onto the card and glue the flowers along the top and bottom.

ACTION-PACKED BIRTHDAY

Young boys who are always on the go will love this action-packed picture card. The design captures the thrills and spills of BMX biking, featuring a photo of a rider on a moving arm, which creates the illusion of him flying through the air. The printed base of the card employs a simple 3D device, but the card will still fold flat for mailing.

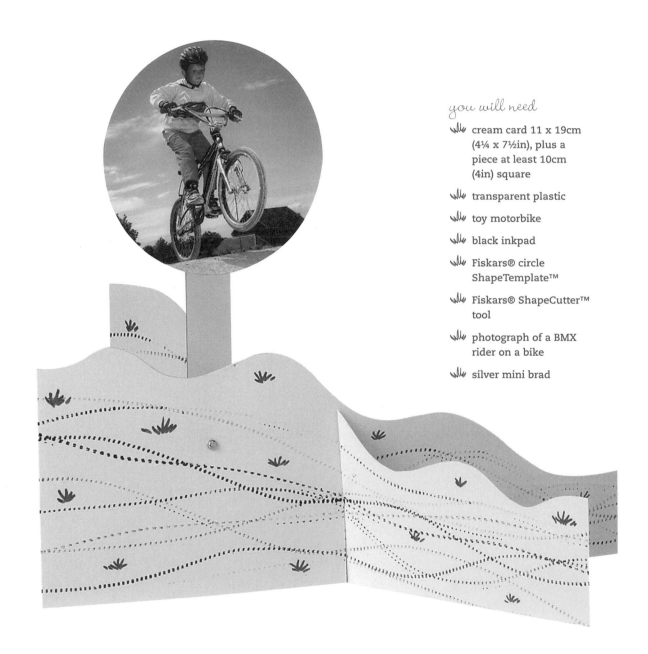

you will need

- cream card 11 x 19cm (4¼ x 7½in), plus a piece at least 10cm (4in) square
- transparent plastic
- toy motorbike
- black inkpad
- Fiskars® circle ShapeTemplate™
- Fiskars® ShapeCutter™ tool
- photograph of a BMX rider on a bike
- silver mini brad

124

Step One
Working on a cutting mat, place the Fiskars® circle ShapeTemplate™, 7.5cm (3in) diameter, over the photograph; use the Fiskars® ShapeCutter™ tool to cut a circle with the image centred. Cut another same-size circle from the cream card square. Apply spray glue to the back of the photograph and stick to the card circle.

Step Two
Using a craft knife against a metal ruler, cut a piece of transparent plastic 12 x 1.5cm (4¾ x ⅝in). Using the point of the craft knife, pierce a small hole in one end of the plastic large enough for the mini brad to be pushed through.

Step Three
Use the template to draw a wavy line across the large piece of cream card (see Templates). Use a craft knife to cut along the line to create two pieces of card with a wavy edge. Cut along the dashed lines as marked on the template. Slot the pieces of cream card together to create an 'X' shape.

Step Four
To make the tyre marks, roll the front wheel of the toy motorbike across the inkpad, then roll it across the cream card, re-inking as necessary. If you cannot find a suitable toy, use a black felt-tip pen to draw the tyre marks freehand.

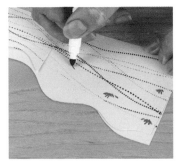

Step Five
Add marks to the cream card with a green felt-tip pen to resemble clumps of grass, applying the pen in an upwards flicking motion.

Step Six
Using adhesive tape, attach the photograph to the end of the plastic without the hole. Using a mini hole punch, punch a hole in the cream card where you want the brad to go. Take the silver mini brad and insert it through the cream card and plastic. Flatten the prongs of the brad out on the wrong side.

tip Source a suitable image from a magazine or the internet, or use a photograph of the birthday boy himself.

Pop-Up Birthday

Stamped balloons cut out and mounted on wire appear to be popping out of the gift with this simple technique.

you will need

- white single fold card 15 x 10cm (6 x 4in)
- yellow, blue and red card
- numbers and striped printed papers
- balloons rubber stamp
- VersaMark™ inkpad
- black embossing powder
- thin silver wire
- very narrow pink ribbon

Cover the base card with a balloon patterned paper. Make a pop-up insert from the numbers printed paper (see The Cardmaker's Basics: Essential Techniques) and glue to the single fold card. Glue a square of striped paper onto the pop-up box and decorate with ribbon tied into a bow. Stamp the balloons onto yellow, blue and red card and heat emboss. Cut the balloons out and layer up using adhesive foam pads. Attach wire coils to the reverse of the stamped balloons and fix to the slits on the inside of the card.

Let's Fly a Kite

The unusual shape of this card, cut from a standard single fold card, shows off the kite and allows it to 'fly'.

you will need

- cream single fold card 15 x 10cm (6 x 4in)
- pale blue, yellow and orange papers
- printed papers in five colours

Cut from the top of the centre fold to the bottom corners of the card to create a triangle; cover with pale blue paper cut to fit. Cut three 5cm (2in) squares from yellow paper and two from orange, and make a teabag folded rosette (see Techniques: Tea Bag Folding). Stick the kite at the top of the card, overlapping the edge. Draw a line snaking down from it using a blue felt-tip pen. Cut two identical 2.5cm (1in) squares of each of the patterned papers, fold them and place together at intervals along the line to make the kite's tail.

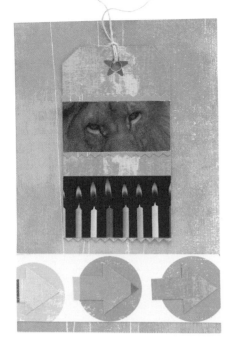

Birthday Surprise

Open this card and slowly unfold the concertina inside to reveal a series of clues to a surprise birthday treat.

you will need
- white single fold card 14 x 8.8cm (5½ x 3½in)
- bold contemporary scrapbook papers
- luggage label
- photo stickers
- zigzag-edge scissors
- string

Cover the front of the card with a printed paper. To make the concertina insert, cut three 15.5 x 22cm (6 x 8¾in) pieces of scrapbook papers. Glue together, overlapping the edges by 1.3cm (½in) and leave to dry. Fold into five equal sections. On the card front decorate the luggage label with a cropped photo sticker relevant to the treat; cut paper arrows to lead into the card. Decorate the pages of the concertina insert with cropped photo stickers to give more clues; for a trip to a safari park for example, use trimmed animal photo stickers – question mark stickers placed alongside the photos will help to build the suspense. The final sticker on the last page of the insert should reveal the surprise, in this case the whole lion's head.

Birthday Boy Biker

If you keep a plentiful supply of themed stickers to hand you will always be able to make a quick card at short notice.

you will need
- silver single fold card 12.5cm (5in) square
- brightly coloured papers
- brad peel-off stickers
- bike and helmet sticker

Cut four rectangles from four brightly coloured papers and stick onto the front of the single fold card so that they frame a small square of silver card in the middle. Stick on the brad peel-off stickers to give the effect that they are holding the panel onto the card. Mount the bike sticker on top. Cut a small yellow tag and decorate with the helmet sticker; thread with string and fix in the top left-hand corner.

PHONE GREETINGS

Teenage girls will love this state-of-the-art mobile (cell) phone card design, with a pink and silver handset that has a visible ringtone and which features a photo of the birthday girl too. The musical notes are made using a simple quilling technique from pink paper edged with metallic pink for extra birthday glitz. For more details on quilling, refer to Techniques: Quilling.

you will need

- ♩ **light pink single fold card 15cm (6in) square**
- ♩ **pink card**
- ♩ **3mm (¹⁄₈in) wide metallic pink-edged pink quilling paper strips**
- ♩ **pink gel pen**
- ♩ **silver stickers – numbers 1–9, two stars, cross, square**
- ♩ **clear dome sticker**
- ♩ **photograph**

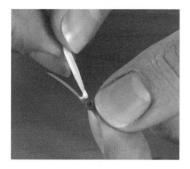

Step One To make a single musical note, tightly coil a 5cm (2in) length of pink paper strip for 4cm (1½in). Remove the tool and glue the end in place. Leave the tail as it is or bend the top over. Make several.

Step Two For the double notes, take a 10cm (4in) length of the pink paper strip and make two folds 4.5cm (1¾in) from either end.

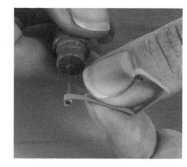

Step Three Make a tight coil in one end and glue in place. Coil the other end in the same direction and glue in place. Repeat to make one more double note.

Step Four Using the pink gel pen, draw a grid of nine boxes for the keypad on a piece of pink card 10 x 5cm (4 x 2in). Add a silver number sticker to each box. Add two stars, a cross and a square sticker above the numbers.

Step Five Take the photo of the birthday girl and place a clear dome sticker over the area you want to use; trim around the edge and glue to the top of the phone.

Step Six Glue the phone to the front of the base card at an angle. Arrange the notes at either side of the top of the phone.

tip In place of a photograph, you could write a text message for the birthday girl.

Birthday Charm

For girls who love to shop, these fun gold charms are a quick way to make an eye-catching birthday card.

you will need

- ♫ pink plastic single fold card 15cm (6in) square
- ♫ pink, red and orange striped paper
- ♫ frames and labels in pink, red and orange
- ♫ five pink and orange flower-shaped brads
- ♫ pink and orange flat back crystals
- ♫ shoe and handbag charms and pink plastic flower
- ♫ narrow purple ribbon

Cut a panel of striped paper: fix a flower-shaped brad in each corner, before securing to the base card with double-sided tape. Stick a frame and three oblong labels in place with adhesive foam pads. Tie the ribbon to the shoe charm and stick inside the frame using an adhesive foam pad. Put a flower brad in the centre hole of the plastic flower; cut a small slit in the square label, push the brad through and open out the legs. Place above the oblong labels. Add the handbag charms, and finish by sticking the flat back crystals in place.

Fashion Girl

The perfect card for fashion-loving girls, the images are stamped directly onto fabric-patterned scrapbook paper.

you will need

- ♫ white single fold card 13 x 10.5cm (5¹⁄₈ x 4¹⁄₈in)
- ♫ white card
- ♫ pink pattern, blue sparkle, heart and fabric-printed scrapbook papers
- ♫ VersaMark™ inkpad
- ♫ blouse, jeans and handbag rubber stamps
- ♫ black embossing powder
- ♫ thin silver wire
- ♫ two pink brads and four clear adhesive gemstones

Stamp the designs onto the fabric-printed papers and heat emboss with black embossing powder; trim close to the outlines and fix the gemstones. Shape a length of wire into a coat hanger and fix behind the blouse with double-sided tape. Cut out a heart; glue onto a pink pattern paper rectangle layered onto white card. Attach brads to the corners and fix onto a panel of pink pattern paper layered onto blue sparkle paper; stick to the base card. Stick on the embellishments with adhesive foam pads.

Sweet Fifteen

Celebrate a girl's 15th birthday with this unusual age card – the 1 is represented by a shimmering lipstick and the 5 is cut from striped paper, both decorated with rhinestones.

you will need

- lilac single fold card 23 x 15.5cm (9 x 6¼in)
- white, light pink, dark pink and lilac paper
- pink striped and printed papers
- silver holographic paper
- tag and small motif stamps
- pink inkpad
- pink and purple rhinestones
- heart punch
- three lilac eyelets

Cover the lower section of the single fold card with pink patterned paper, and attach a narrow border strip to the top of the card. Use the templates (see Templates) to cut a number 1 from dark pink paper topped with silver holographic paper and a number 5 from pink striped paper. Highlight with rhinestones and add a pink punched heart to the lipstick. Stick the numbers in the centre of the lilac card. Stamp the tags onto light pink and lilac paper and cut out. Attach in place with the eyelets.

Gift Box

The stamp used for this card features a fold line so that once the stamped box is folded and assembled the lid can pop-up to reveal a hidden message.

Stamp the image onto the large dotty paper and heat emboss. Repeat this process on two pieces of pink card and set aside. Cut out the image on the dotty paper and fold along the marked lines. Glue scrunched up tissue paper under the lid. Cut out the ribbon and bow from one piece of stamped pink card, and just the bow from the other. Glue the ribbon onto the box, then layer the bow onto the present using adhesive foam pads. Cut a simple tag shape from a scrap of pink card and add a punched heart. Glue the completed gift box to the centre of the card.

you will need

- orange sponged-effect single fold card 21 x 14.5cm (8¼ x 5¾in)
- surprise package rubber stamp
- VersaMark™ inkpad
- black embossing powder
- large dotty scrapbook paper
- orange tissue paper
- small heart punch

SOCCER FAN

Any soccer-mad teenage boy will love this action-packed birthday card that has some real bounce. Its dynamic design has been created with simple peel-off stickers and coils of silver wire to give the impression of the soccer balls in motion. The strong, graphic elements and colour contrast add to the overall impact.

you will need

- ✪ green single fold card 11.5 x 18cm (4½ x 7in)
- ✪ white card
- ✪ dark green card 2 x 18cm (¾ x 7in)
- ✪ light green card 7 x 18cm (2¾ x 7in)
- ✪ soccer ball and soccer player peel-off stickers
- ✪ 24-gauge silver wire
- ✪ pliers
- ✪ fancy-edged scissors

Step One Stick four soccer balls onto white card and carefully cut around each one. Here, three sizes of ball are used: two large, one medium and one small.

Step Two Using the pliers, cut a 12cm (4¾in) length of wire. Using your hands and the natural coil of the wire, twist it to make small loops. Cut one 10cm (4in) and two 8cm (3¼in) lengths and make three more looped pieces in the same way. Using adhesive tape, attach one piece of looped wire to the wrong side of each cut out ball.

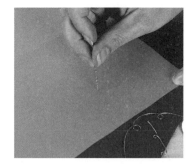

Step Three Open out the green single fold card and place right side up on a foam pad. Prick a hole in the centre front of the card about 5cm (2in) from one short edge, then prick another hole 1cm (⅜in) below it. Make three more holes about 2.5cm (1in) apart along the centre front of the card. Make three more holes 1cm (⅜in) underneath these so that you have four pairs of holes.

Step Four Insert the end of one looped wire into the top hole of one pair of holes, then thread it through the lower hole. Secure the end in place with adhesive tape. Trim any excess wire with the pliers. Repeat with the other looped wires and pairs of holes.

Step Five Using the fancy-edged scissors, cut along the dark green card 5mm (³⁄₁₆in) away from one long edge. Glue this edged strip along the bottom of the light green card.

Step Six Choose four soccer player peel-off stickers and position evenly spaced along the light green card. Using adhesive foam pads, mount this decorated card panel to cover the taped ends of the wire.

tip You could choose the colours of the recipient's favourite soccer team and theme the card accordingly.

Skateboard Sliders

A simple moving device – the slider bar – has been used to capture the spirit of the sport of skateboarding.

you will need

- white single fold card, 15 x 20cm (6 x 8in)
- white card
- grey paper
- brick and green flock dolls' house paper
- skateboard stickers

Glue the brick paper to the front of the single fold card. Cut the slope from grey paper and the slider bar from white card (see Templates). Glue the slope to the bottom edge and a strip of green flock paper on top. Glue the white card slider bar to grey paper and cut out. Open up the card and cut two vertical slots in the grey slope near the left edge 1cm (3/8in) apart and slightly longer than the width of the bar. Insert the slider bar into the slots. Stick a skateboarder sticker to the end of the slider, trimming off the excess card showing behind the sticker. Stick more skateboarders on the background wall.

Motorbike Trio

Young motorbike enthusiasts will be impressed by this spectacle of a succession of rubber-stamped racers dramatically leaning over to take a tight corner.

you will need

- mid and light blue card
- motorbike rubber stamp
- black inkpad
- circle cutting tool

Score and fold a rectangle of mid blue card into a concertina. Stamp the motorbike onto light blue card three times. Use a circle cutting tool to cut a 7.5cm (3in) diameter circle around each stamped image. Colour in and stick onto mid blue card circles cut slightly larger. Glue each circle centrally over the mountain folds of the concertina card.

Formula 1

This novelty card is perfect for all those young Lewis Hamiltons out there.

you will need

- red single fold card 14.5cm (5¾in) square
- yellow card 11 x 14.5cm (4¼ x 5¾in)
- black, red, yellow and blue card
- black checked paper
- three racing car peel-off stickers
- silver pen
- circle punch 1.5cm (⅝in) diameter
- circle punch 2.8cm (1¹/₁₆in) diameter

Stick the peel-off stickers on red, yellow and blue card and cut out. Punch out four small circles from black card, leaving a 3cm (1¹/₈in) space between each. Insert the black card into the large circle punch so that the smaller circle is in the centre and punch out. Draw small marks for the tread around the outside edges of the 'tyres'. Cut a circuit and flag (see Templates) from black card. Decorate the flag with checked paper. Attach the yellow card panel to the base card and use double-sided tape to fix the circuit, two cars and flag in place. Glue the final car and the tyres overlapping on the red strip at the base of the card.

Rock Star

A very quick card to make for budding rock stars, using layered card panels and peel-off stickers.

you will need

- silver single fold card 10 x 15cm (4 x 6in)
- gold, red and white card
- gold musical notes and instruments peel-off stickers

Stick your chosen instrument peel-off stickers to white card and colour in with red and black felt-tip pens. Cut out and mount onto a red card panel together with peel-off microphones. Mount the red card onto a slightly larger piece of gold card, then fix to the silver single fold card. To create a lively patterned border fix gold-edged black musical note peel-off stickers all around the edges of the card.

DIY BIRTHDAY

This is the ideal card for the home-improvement enthusiast. It is a perfect example of a shaker card, a design that emits an intriguing rattle before it is opened. The secret is in the foam box frame with a clear acetate window that is fixed to the front of the card. It is filled with a mixture of real washers and silver card washers. The 'tools' are ready-made stickers and relief stickers.

you will need

- red single fold card 15cm (6in) square
- yellow card 14cm (5½in) square
- red card 9cm (3½in) square
- red self-adhesive foam 8.5cm (3³⁄8in) square
- shiny silver card A5 (8 x 6in) sheet
- acetate 8.5cm (3³⁄8in) square
- circle craft punches – 12mm (½in) and 8mm (³⁄8in)
- eyelet hole punches – 4mm (¹⁄8in) and 8mm (³⁄8in)
- DIY-theme stickers
- fine silver glitter
- 12 small silver metal washers

Step One Cut a 6.5cm (2½in) aperture centrally in the small red card square and the self-adhesive foam square. Glue the yellow card square to the front of the base card. Lightly mark the position of the shaker box. Apply a thin layer of glue over the non-adhesive side of the red foam frame and glue in place. Do not remove the backing paper from the foam yet.

Step Two Brush glue thinly over the wrong side of the card frame and press the acetate on top. Remove any excess adhesive prior to sticking to prevent glue oozing out onto the acetate window. Allow to dry.

Step Three Punch out fifteen 8mm (⅜in) and fifteen 12mm (½in) silver card circles. Use a 3mm (⅛in) hole punch to remove the centres from all the smaller circles and a 8mm (⅜in) hole punch for the larger ones. Add the card washers to the shaker well (ensuring that the silver side is uppermost) and four of the metal washers.

Step Four Peel the backing paper from the foam frame and press the acetate frame on top, trapping the washers inside.

Step Five Enliven the DIY-theme stickers by gluing glitter to all the silver parts. Allow to dry. For added dimension, turn the saw, hammer and screwdriver into relief stickers. Use the tweezers to hold each sticker and then fix in place with adhesive foam pads.

Step Six Remove the remaining stickers from the sheet one by one with the tweezers and press onto the card. Add further interest to the design by gluing on the remaining metal washers.

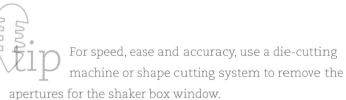

tip For speed, ease and accuracy, use a die-cutting machine or shape cutting system to remove the apertures for the shaker box window.

you will need

- dark orange single fold card 10.7 x 23cm (4¼ x 9in)
- light orange card
- gardening stickers
- light green and green checked paper
- orange 3mm (1/8in) wide quilling paper strips
- green 1cm (3/8in) wide quilling paper strips
- quilling tool
- eight orange and one green square brads
- string

His Vegetable Patch

The perfect card for a gardening enthusiast featuring gardening motifs and a quilled bunch of carrots.

Cut a panel of light orange card slightly smaller than the single fold card. Cut three pieces of green paper. Decorate two pieces with gardening stickers. Glue the third piece onto green checked paper cut slightly larger. Attach to the base card, leaving a border around the edge and equal spaces in between. Fix the brads. Make three quilled carrots (see Techniques: Quilling). Tie string around the middle of the carrots and fix onto the centre panel.

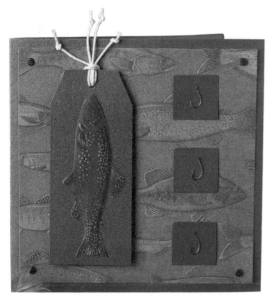

Birthday Catch

An angler's dream – this card design uses fish-themed embossed card and paper vellum.

Make a copper card tag. Cut a fish from the vellum and mount onto the tag using a glue pen. Make a hole and thread string through. Cut a square of embossed card slightly smaller than the single fold card to leave a narrow border all the way round. Using a brad at each corner, fix the embossed card panel to the main card. Cut three squares from the copper card, stick a fishing hook to each one, and attach to the right-hand side of the card with double-sided tape. Use adhesive foam pads to stick the tag in place.

you will need

- copper single fold card 15cm (6in) square
- extra copper card
- fish embossed vellum and card
- embellishments – brads, fishing hooks, string

tip Bend and shape small lengths of silver wire with round-nosed pliers to make your own fish hooks.

Batsman's Birthday

Devoted cricket fans will be bowled over by this all-action image using the technique of 3D découpage.

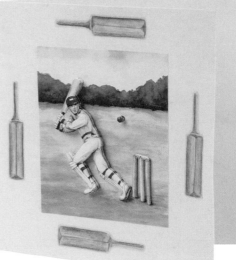

you will need
- cream single fold card 15cm (6in) square
- white card
- cricket découpage papers
- cricket bat outline stamp
- light brown inkpad
- black and brown watercolour pencils
- silicone gel and tweezers with locking device

Stamp the cricket bat outline stamp around the edge of the base card. Colour in using black and brown watercolour pencils. More brown pencil was applied to one side of the bat and more black to the same side of the handle, to give the bat some dimension. Blend the coloured pencils with a damp paintbrush. Once dry, glue a 3D découpage panel made from the cricket découpage papers in the centre (see Techniques: 3D Découpage for how to make the panel).

Big Birthday Balloons

Big birthdays aren't always bad news, so send him off on the next stage of life's great adventure with this bright and breezy design.

you will need
- yellow embossed single fold card 18 x 11.5cm (7 x 4½in)
- green card
- blue, orange, red, purple and pink 3mm (⅛in) wide quilling paper strips
- quilling tool
- green number peel-off stickers
- silver pen

Attach the number peel-off stickers to a small square of green card. Using adhesive foam pads, attach to the bottom front of the base card and decorate with a tiny tag. To make a balloon, glue two 40cm (16in) lengths of paper strip end to end to create a length 80cm (32in) long and make a loose closed coil and pinch to a teardrop shape (see Techniques: Quilling). Place PVA (white) glue over one side and attach. Draw silver pen lines from each balloon to the green card square. To finish the balloon, make a loose closed coil from a 15cm (6in) length of quilling paper and pinch into a triangle shape.

DREAMBOAT

If it is his dream to sail off into the sunset, the birthday man will love this stylish card. This smart, shipshape design, complete with a seaman's trusty reef knot tied through eyelets for a simple yet stylish effect, is decorated with a gold heat-embossed yacht. You will need to make a card box to send this in and for more details see Techniques: Making Envelopes.

you will need

- blue single fold card 10cm (4in) square
- pale blue hammer-textured folded card 14.5cm (5¾in) square
- Magic Motifs™ 'Sailing'
- gold embossing powder
- two 15cm (6in) and two 18cm (7in) lengths of white cord
- eight gold eyelets

Step One Cut around the yacht image; remove the clear backing sheet and place in the centre of the blue card square. Press down; remove the white front sheet to leave the transparent image on the blue card. Sprinkle gold embossing powder over to cover entirely. Shake off the excess.

Step Two Hold a corner of the card with a wooden clothes peg and hold over a ceramic tile to protect your work surface. Using a heat gun, heat the embossing powder until it melts and becomes semi-liquid. Be careful not to overheat as the gold will tarnish.

Step Three Punch two holes, about 3mm (⅛in) apart, in each corner of the blue card. Turn the card over (right side down); insert a gold eyelet into each hole and set.

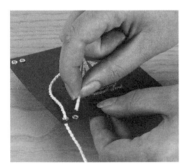

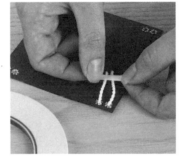

Step Four From the wrong side, insert one shorter length of white cord through an eyelet hole in the bottom left-hand corner of the card and then back out through the eyelet hole next to it, to form a loop on the right side.

Step Five Using adhesive tape, secure the ends of the white cord to the wrong side of the card.

Step Six Thread one longer piece of white cord from the wrong side up through an eyelet hole in the top left-hand corner, up through the loop, around the back of the loop, back down through the loop and down through the other eyelet hole; secure. Repeat on the right-hand side of the card so that the knots are staggered. Mount onto the base card using adhesive foam pads.

tip Instead of a Magic Motif™, you can use an embossing pen to draw a yacht shape, or use a rubber stamp with a sailing motif and an embossing inkpad.

Flying Colours

Keen sailors will love this quilled design, but if time is short cut the flags from coloured card.

you will need

- dark blue single fold card 10 x 15cm (4 x 6in)
- blue cord and four gold eyelets
- mid blue card
- yellow, black, white, bright blue and red 3mm (1/8in) wide quilling paper strips

Glue a mid blue card panel to the centre of the single fold card. Punch a double set of holes at either side and fix the eyelets. Thread through a length of cord and glue in place. Make six flags from the quilling papers (see Techniques: Quilling for how to make different quilled shapes). Stick the flags in place beneath the cord. To finish, tie short lengths of the cord into a sailing knot and fix to the bottom right-hand corner.

Celtic Celebration

The style stone embellishment, with its engraved Celtic design, complements the stamped background beautifully.

you will need

- dark blue single fold card 12.5cm (5in) square
- silver card
- dark blue paper
- Celtic panel and border rubber stamps
- blue Crafter's™ inkpad
- dark blue inkpad
- VersaMark™ inkpad
- green pearlescent powder
- style stone, thin wire and pearl beads

Sponge the single fold card with dark blue ink to create a criss-cross pattern. Stamp the Celtic designs onto dark blue paper using the light blue ink. Use a ruler to tear Celtic border strips and glue to the card. Cut out the Celtic panel design and fix to a silver card square cut slightly larger; attach to the base card on point. Sponge dark blue ink into the style stone's recessed design, then stamp with the Celtic panel stamp; attach to the card with thin wire, doubled up and threaded with beads.

tip For extra shimmer emboss all the Celtic patterns with a green pearlescent powder.

Winning Hand

Card-players will love this birthday card that has real 3D appeal.

you will need

- red single fold card 10 x 12.5cm (4 x 5in)
- red and white card
- printed paper
- red and black 3mm (¹/8in) wide quilling paper strips
- quilling tool
- number and letter rub-ons

Make loose closed coils using 3mm (¹/8in) red and black paper strips and pinch and arrange to form the spade, club, heart and diamond shapes (see Techniques: Quilling). Glue in place on four playing cards that have been cut from white card. Use the number and letter rub-ons to decorate the corners of the cards. Embellish a strip of red card with printed paper and mount onto the front of the base card with adhesive foam pads to form a pocket. Tuck the playing cards into the pocket, fan out and glue in place.

Birthday Chef

Celebrate your man's culinary accomplishments with this composition of a cook's essentials.

you will need

- blue single fold card 19 x 16cm (7½ x 6¼in)
- blue, mid blue and silver card
- mid blue 2mm (³/32in) wide quilling paper strips
- light blue, white, red checked, dark blue, dark blue striped and floral papers
- mini wooden rolling pin

Cut a square of light blue paper slightly smaller than the single fold card and glue in place. Cut two small squares of red checked paper, two slightly smaller squares of blue card, and one square of light blue paper, slightly smaller again. Cut the saucepan from silver card, the apron from striped paper and a pair of oven mitts from floral paper (see Templates). Add a pocket, neck loop and waist ties to the apron. Make the hat from a piece of pleated white paper finished with a folded band at the base. Mount all the elements in place following the photograph.

HAT STACK

A woman can never have enough hats. A charming rubber stamp
is the start point for this very pretty card design and the hat motif
is continued with the careful selection of complementary dies.
Restricting the design to using only the shades of a single colour
creates a simple yet sophisticated birthday greeting.

you will need

- light blue card
  13 x 20cm (5 x 8in)
  plus scraps
- white linen-effect
  card
- mid blue and dark
  blue card
- scraps of printed
  papers
- chick and hats
  rubber stamp
- royal blue
  VersaColor™ inkpad
- pearl blue embossing
  powder
- blue glaze pen
- die-cutting tool and
  hat dies
- narrow blue ribbon
- very narrow checked
  blue ribbon

144

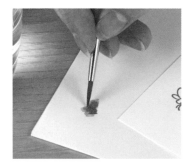

Step One Using the inkpad, ink the chick stamp up carefully. Check that there is ink all over the image, then stamp onto the white linen-effect card.

Step Two Sprinkle the embossing powder all over the wet stamped image. Tip away the excess powder, returning it to the jar. Check that the image is completely covered and carefully remove any stray powder with a paintbrush. Using a heat gun, heat the surface of the powder (see Techniques: Heat Embossing).

Step Three Run the glaze pen over scrap paper – the flow will be quicker than on plastic, and speed is of the essence, as you must use the ink before it dries out. Dip a fine paintbrush into clean water and pick up some of the ink. Test the intensity of the diluted colour on scrap paper.

Step Four Starting with one section at a time, such as the chick, flower or one of the hats, apply a light wash to one side to create shading. This will make them look more 3D. When returning to a section to add more shading, pick up less water and more ink.

Step Five Apply very light colour washes in patches to the background, leaving a white halo around the image. Apply a little more colour below the chick for ground. Trim the card to 10 x 7.5cm (4 x 3in). Stick the narrow blue ribbon across the bottom. Mount on a slightly larger piece of mid blue card.

Step Six Score and fold two flaps 5cm (2in) wide at either side of the light blue card. Fix the stamped panel inside. Die-cut and assemble two hats from dark and light blue card and printed papers. Mount one on the inside and the other on the left-hand flap with an adhesive foam pad. Glue the checked ribbon to the card back, to tie in front.

tip Apply a little extra pressure when stamping on slightly textured card to compensate for the unevenness of the surface and to avoid losing parts of the print.

Shop Till She Drops

Make fashion accessories from quilled circles
and teardrops for glamorous girlfriends.

you will need

- blue single fold
  card 10 x 15cm
  (4 x 6in)
- gold, blue and
  floral printed
  papers
- blue 3mm (1/8in)
  wide quilling
  paper strips
- quilling tool
- small gemstones
- gold gel pen

Draw small shoe and bag shapes on scrap paper and use them to cut a bag and a shoe
from blue paper. Quill a selection of circles and teardrops in varying sizes (see Techniques:
Quilling); fit onto the shapes and glue. Stick the quilled shapes to circles of floral paper.
Add tight circles to make a handle for the bag, and gemstones to the bag centre and top
of the shoe. Quill teardrops for the earrings and tight circles for the ring and necklace;
stick onto smaller circles of floral paper and finish with gold pen and gemstones. Stick the
decorated circles on top of slightly larger gold paper circles and glue to the card.

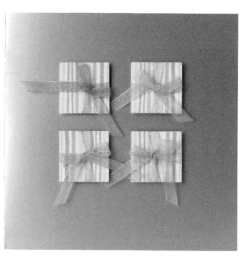

Birthday Presents

A very easy card that can be made in just a few
minutes when a birthday takes you by surprise.

you will need

- silver single fold card
  15cm (6in) square
- white card
- striped paper
- narrow lilac, blue, green
  and pink pastel sheer ribbon

Cut four squares from the striped paper and stick to white card
using double-sided tape; trim around the edges. Wrap each
parcel with a different coloured length of ribbon and tie in a bow.
Mount the parcels on the front of the silver card using adhesive
foam pads.

Pretty Purse

This pretty purse card is created by using a special
iris stamp, which includes the folding pattern.

you will need

- aqua single fold card
  12.5cm (5in) square
- pink and gold card
- bright floral paper pack

- purse stamp
- VersaMark™ inkpad
- gold embossing powder

Stamp the image onto a 9.5cm (3¾in) square of pink card and heat emboss with gold embossing powder. Cut the
centre aperture from the stamped image. Turn the image face down and place the cut out centre face up within
the aperture so that the folding pattern can be followed. Cut three sheets of the floral paper into 4cm (1½in) strips;
fold in half and follow the pattern (see Techniques: Iris Folding). Once complete, turn the card over and remove the
centre template; stick onto gold card using adhesive foam pads, then onto the base card using double-sided tape.

Birthday Bubbles

A birthday is a cause for celebration so break out the champagne with
this bubbly card combining masking, stamping and die-cut techniques.

you will need

- pink pearlescent single fold
  card 21 x 10cm (8¼ x 4in)
- white, light yellow, light pink
  and light green card
- mouse on a champagne cork
  rubber stamp
- pink, canary and cyan
  VersaColor™ inkpads

- graphite black Brilliance™ inkpad
- green, brown, black and pink
  brush markers
- die-cutting tool; small, medium
  and large bubbles, and champagne
  bottle dies
- holographic glitter glue

Decorate the base card using the die-cut bubbles as a mask (see The Cardmaker's
Basics). Using the black inkpad, stamp the mouse onto white card. Colour in with
the brush markers diluted with water. Stick onto yellow card and trim to angle the
sides. Mount onto the base card with adhesive foam pads. Sponge yellow, blue
and pink ink over spare die-cut bubbles. Die cut and assemble a champagne bottle
from yellow, pink and green card, and sponge highlights. Arrange and mount the
bubbles and bottle with adhesive foam pads. Add glitter glue highlights to finish.

VIBRANT ROSES

Flowers make the perfect motif to celebrate a woman's birthday and this Art Nouveau-style stamp design is ideal. The vibrant jewel-like colours of the roses provide a perfect contrast to the metal foil. Stamping on metal foil, with its non-porous surface, requires permanent ink, such as the StazOn™ inkpad used here, and its smoothness demands a controlled stamping technique.

you will need

- white linen-effect folded card 14.5cm (5¾in) square
- green lightweight metal foil
- rose garden and single rose rubber stamps
- jet black StazOn™ inkpad
- deep pink and green OHP (over-head-projector) pens
- black outline tags, eyelets, lines and squares peel-off stickers
- four black 3mm (⅛in) eyelets

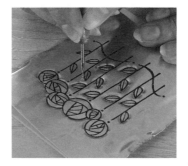

Step One
Using the black inkpad, stamp the rose garden on a square piece of foil larger than the image (to allow for tearing) and two single roses on pieces slightly larger than the tag peel-off stickers. The ink will dry within a few minutes of stamping, but a heat gun can quicken the process.

Step Two
Place the foil on a foam mat and, using the fine ball on a dual embossing tool, draw a broken line around the flower heads and leaves to emphasize the design (on the outside of the stamped line and not directly on top). Using a ruler and the other end of the embossing tool, draw straight broken lines down the sides of the stems.

Step Three
Colour in the flower heads and leaves. On the flower heads, colour from the centre outwards, as this avoids any buckling. As the foil is quite soft, the pens will push it down, adding to the effect.

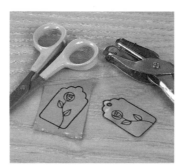

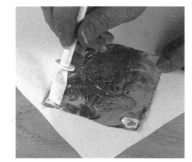

Step Four
Tear away some of the background around the rose garden panel – the foil is soft enough to tear by hand. If you experience any difficulty starting to tear, make a small cut with scissors. Alternatively, use fancy-edged scissors.

Step Five
Lift a peel-off outline tag from the sheet and let it spring back to shape. Hover above one of the single roses to select the chosen area for the tag. Place in position and repeat for the second tag. Make a hole in the top of both tags. Position an eyelet peel-off sticker over each hole. Cut out. Colour in and make a tie for each tag with a peel-off line.

Step Six
Apply PVA (white) glue on the corners of the foil panel. Mount the foil slightly towards the top of the white single fold card. Punch a hole in each corner of the foil panel and fix an eyelet in each. Place three little squares on the right-hand side. Stick one of the tags overlapping the left-hand edge. Using adhesive foam pads, mount the second tag below overlapping the first.

A Gift for You

Who could resist this pretty little 'gift' card. With its perfectly tied bow, it makes the ideal birthday card.

you will need

- orange single fold card 15 x 10cm (6 x 4in) plus extra
- orange marker and glaze pens
- fuchsia pink satin ribbon

To make the 'gift box' lid, cut a strip of orange card slightly wider than the single fold card. To add a simple pattern to the base card, draw diagonal lines first with the orange marker pen, then draw across again with the orange glaze pen. Add a border to the lid too. Tie the ribbon with a double-loop bow at the top to finish.

birthays ◎ more for WOMEN

Beautiful Blooms

This spray of fringed and coiled flowers makes a highly attractive and innovative 3D card design.

you will need

- two-fold lilac card 18 x 12.5cm (7 x 4^{7}/$_{8}$in) with oval aperture
- light yellow 1cm (^{3}/$_{8}$in) wide quilling paper strips
- dark yellow and light green 3mm (^{1}/$_{8}$in) wide quilling paper strips
- fringing and quilling tool
- purple card

Mount a panel of purple card behind the oval aperture. Make five fringed and coiled flowers (see Techniques: Quilling). Apply a dab of glue to the underside of each flower and attach to the purple panel trimming as necessary. To make the leaves, cut three lengths of light green paper strip in varying sizes. Trim one end of each to a point. Run a fingernail along the lengths to slightly stretch and curl them. Glue to the flower stems.

tip Any number of flowers in a single colour, or a mixture, could be used to make a bouquet.

Birthday Butterflies

This very pretty card makes use of the technique of tea bag folding for the lovely golden butterflies.

you will need

- cream single fold card 18.5 x 7cm (7¼ x 2¾in)
- gold and floral vellum paper
- gold 3D paint
- gold gel pen

Cut a 2.5cm (1in) wide strip of floral vellum and a slightly wider strip of gold vellum. Stick the floral strip on top of the gold, then stick both onto the single fold card. Cut and fold ten 2.5cm (1in) gold vellum squares (see Techniques: Tea Bag Folding, Steps 1–5). Pair up with points together to form butterfly shapes and stick to the card. Use gold 3D paint to create the heads and bodies. Finally, draw on the antennae using the gold gel pen.

Bearing Gifts

Use a printed background paper as a guide to colouring a central stamped design to achieve a coordinated look to your card.

you will need

- white linen-effect single fold card 12.5cm (5in) square
- blue and smooth white card
- multi-coloured striped paper
- four red brads
- teddy bear and flowers rubber stamp
- graphite black Brilliance™ inkpad
- yellow, orange, spring green, red and blue brush markers

Cover the single fold card with striped paper. Stamp the teddy bear and flowers image onto smooth white card and colour in with the brush markers. Trim the card to 7cm (2¾in) square and mount onto a slightly larger square of blue card. Punch a hole in each corner with a 1.5mm (¹/₁₆in) hole punch and insert the brads. Mount the panel onto the base card with adhesive foam pads.

 tip To make the envelope shown, see Techniques: Making Envelopes.

Techniques

This section has handy step-by-step guides to all the essential techniques you will need to make the cards featured in this book. Long after you have made and given the cards, this section will prove indispensable as you create designs of your own. For each of the featured techniques, there is information on tools and materials required, essential skills, as well as creative options for you to explore.

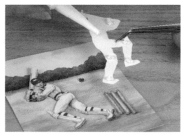

STAMPING

This is one of the easiest ways to add decoration to a card while achieving a professional-looking result. A pre-cut design is mounted onto a block, making it easy to handle. The stamp is inked up, usually with an inkpad, then pressed to transfer it to your chosen surface. Although the design can be printed over and over again, there are so many ways to be creative including different colour choice options and exciting printing effects.

TYPES OF STAMP

Stamps come in all shapes and sizes. All stamps have a die, which can be made of rubber, polymer or foam and incorporates the image. Stamps are sold individually or in sets, generally on a theme.

SOLID STAMPS

These print the image as a block without leaving any areas to be coloured in. They are excellent for creating backgrounds and can be enhanced by applying colour directly onto the die, with brush markers for example.

OUTLINE STAMPS

These print only the outline of the image, leaving blank areas that can be coloured in.

CLEAR STAMPS

The clear dies come as a set, stored between two plastic sheets. One of the sheets is printed with the designs contained within the set. This is the storage base to which you should always return the dies. The other plastic sheet covers and protects the dies.

It is important to select the right type of ink for the surface you are stamping. Most come with guidance on use, but it is always wise to do a test print. Available in a variety of sizes and shapes, most inkpads have a raised sponge or felt pad that makes it easy to ink up any size of stamp. Some come in single colours, while others are multicoloured.

DYE-BASED INKS

These are water-based, mainly non-permanent and usually have a felt pad. They are available in a variety of colours, including multicoloured or 'rainbow' pads. Dye-based inks such as Kaleidacolor™ are translucent, dry quickly and can be stamped on most types of paper, but work best on glossy paper. When a permanent finish is required, when working on style stones for example, a brand such as Ancient Page™ works well.

The Caribbean Kaleidacolor™ is an example of a multicoloured dye-based inkpad. To avoid the inks running into each other, the bands of colour are divided into mini inkpads, which, when ready to be used, can be made to slide together by pushing the notch.

PIGMENT INKS

These are thick, creamy and opaque, and usually come with a foam pad. They are available in a multitude of sizes and colours. Some, such as Brilliance™ and Mica Magic™, are fast drying, making them ideal to use on a variety of unusual surfaces such as vellum and shrink plastic. For heat embossing, however, choose slow-drying pigment ink such as Versacolor™ or ColorBox™.

EMBOSSING INKS

Clear or slightly tinted, most embossing inks come with a foam pad. They are designed to dry slowly so that you can use them with opaque, glitter or metallic embossing powders.

RESIST INKS

These are formulated to resist or repel water-based dye inks on glossy paper. The VersaMark™ can be used to create a watermark or tone-on-tone effect. It also acts as 'glue' for chalks and paint powders.

RE-INKING YOUR INKPADS

Replace the inkpad lid immediately after use or it will dry out. Never throw away dry inkpads. Re-inkers are available for most inkpads; these are small bottles of ink that you can use to bring your inkpads back to life. Always try to re-ink your inkpads as evenly as possible.

PERMANENT/SOLVENT INKS

Permanent inks are available in both water- and solvent-based forms and can be used on most types of card as well as other surfaces such as acetate, shrink plastic, metal foil and acrylic. You may need a special stamp cleaner to remove solvent inks from your stamps, and these inks should always be used in a well-ventilated area.

A solvent-based ink such as StazOn™ is fast drying permanent ink that is ideal for stamping onto the smooth, non-porous surface of acetate, as it does not need to be heated to be fixed.

1 Squeeze the bottle gently to apply the ink evenly over the entire surface of the inkpad.

2 Use a piece of thick card to drag across any ink still on the surface of the inkpad until it has been soaked up.

tip Store dye-based inkpads with a felt pad upside down, so that the ink travels to the pad surface and doesn't dry out.

Perfect the art of inking and printing, and learn how to get the best results from both rubber and clear stamps. Have lots of scrap paper ready and practise your printing technique until you get the right results.

USING AN INKPAD

The primary technique of stamping from an inkpad is crucial to master if you want to produce crisp images. It is important to work on a perfectly flat surface.

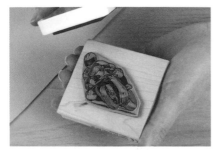

1 Inkpads are often smaller than the stamp, but this is not a problem. Hold the stamp design side up. Take a single-colour inkpad and dab it over the design. Dab the inkpad over the design several times to apply an even coating of ink. (Do not press the inkpad against the rubber or too much ink may be released onto the surface.) Remove any ink from the edges of the stamp (caused by overinking) with a paper towel.

2 Grip the wooden mount of the stamp on either side with your fingers. Press it, rubber-side down, onto the card using firm, even, downward pressure. Try not to rock the stamp. The larger the stamp, the more pressure you need to apply. Gently lift up the stamp away from the card and check the printed image left on the surface. Let the print dry naturally before handling. To quicken the process, a heat gun can be used.

3 Clean your stamps immediately after use by placing two pieces of damp kitchen paper on a saucer and pressing the stamp onto the paper several times. Dry the stamp with clean, dry kitchen paper. If necessary you can use a soft toothbrush to scrub away the residue from the recesses of your stamp.

If a stamp is considerably smaller than the inkpad you are using, you can tap it directly onto the surface of the pad.

tip Some inks, such as solvent inks, require a special stamp cleaner.

When applying ink to a large stamp, a brayer is a good way to ensure an even coating of ink.

BACKGROUND STAMPING

When stamping a background, protect your work surface by placing the card on a piece of scrap paper and stamp over the edges of the card for a professional result. Re-ink the die between each print, and alter the angle of each print to add interest to the pattern.

techniques ◎ STAMPING

USING BRUSH MARKERS

If you wish to produce a stamped image using different colours – an orange flower with a green stem, for example – special coloured brush markers are the answer. Simply colour each area of the stamp and then press onto the paper or card. You'll find it helps if you breathe over the stamp before you press it in place to ensure that the ink is wet because these markers can dry quickly.

tip You can also use brush markers to colour up and print selected areas of the stamp only, such as a flower without the stem.

USING CLEAR STAMPS

Clear stamps are are very easy to use, take up very little storage space and are good value for money. The dies are generally made from a transparent polymer that you mount onto a clear acrylic block to create a stamp that you can see through. This enables you to stamp with great precision. In addition, they allow you to combine different elements or images and colours with ease, so that you can compose and create your own individual designs. Once you have finished stamping, always clean the dies and blocks straight away in soapy water to revive their clinging power. Use a small bowl for small dies to keep from losing them down the plughole.

APPLYING COLOUR TO STAMPED IMAGES

You have seen how your stamp can be inked up with a pad or special marker pens, but the stamped image can also be coloured in after it is printed. Paints can also be used either for detail colouring or to apply an overall wash. If you intend to colour the stamped image with paints or felt-tip markers, make sure you use a pad with permanent ink to ensure that the outline won't smudge or bleed. For a softer look, chalks can be used; apply to larger areas with a cotton wool ball and to detail areas with a cotton bud.

When using brush markers to colour in a stamped design with two shades of the same colour, use the lightest colour first to avoid contaminating the pen nibs; use the wetness of the pens to blend the colours where they meet.

To use brush markers for a more painterly effect, run each brush marker over a plastic lid. Dip a fine paintbrush into clean water, pick up some of the ink and fill in the image; apply also to the background for depth, as shown in this detail from the Bearing Gifts card (Birthdays).

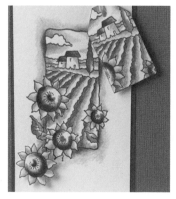

When using colour pencils to colour in stamped images, shading and blending is achieved by simply varying the pressure on the tip (French Leave card, Life's Special Moments).

techniques ◉ STAMPING

Once you have gained in skill and confidence in stamping on card and paper, you can explore stamping on other materials to add a new dimension to your stamped card designs.

METAL

Tin metals or thin sheets of metal foil are suitable to stamp on. Metal foil comes in different thicknesses. Thicker foil, although more sturdy, is not so easy for drawing into. Lightweight foil is thin enough to punch, cut with scissors (straight- or fancy-edged) and tear. Stamping on metal foil, with its non-porous surface, requires permanent ink, and its smoothness requires a controlled stamping technique. Any movement once the stamp is in contact with the foil will cause the image to blur, so the minimum amount of pressure is needed.

SHRINK PLASTIC

Available in translucent and opaque white, clear, cream and black sheets, shrink plastic can be stamped, coloured, cut out and baked to make embellishments for your cards. It sometimes comes pre-sanded on one side. If not, you will need to sand it before stamping to give the ink a texture on which to key; use an extra-fine grade paper wrapped around a sanding block with a circular motion.

ACETATE

Acetate is a thin, transparent plastic that comes in sheets ready to use. The smooth, non-porous surface of acetate requires special ink that will dry permanently, but not all acetate is heat resistant, so check or experiment before using a heat gun to emboss or set the ink. Acetate allows you to layer stamped images on top of each other.

STYLE STONES

These are inkable, cultured stones that come in two finishes, coated and natural. The coated stones are ivory in colour and have flat surfaces that are ideal for precise stamping and colour blending. The natural stones are white in colour and have engraved surfaces. These are ideal for simple stamped designs and colouring. They come in a variety of shapes including tags, frames and hearts.

POLYMER CLAY

Fimo™ and Sculpey™ are just two types of polymer clay that can be stamped to produce imprints. They are easy to use and can be baked in an ordinary oven. The clay should be rolled out smoothly until it is about 3mm (1/8in) thick, so that the image can be stamped evenly. Press the stamp firmly into the surface of the clay. When stamping onto clay you need to apply more pressure than you would to stamp onto paper.

1 Handprint stamps are mounted together side by side on the acrylic block. The more pressure applied, the deeper and more effective the cast will be.

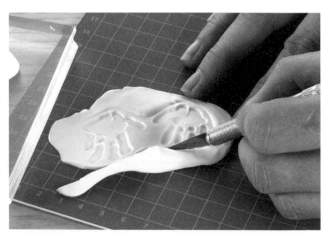

2 Cut around the edges of the clay and bake in an oven following the manufacturer's instructions.

MAKING YOUR OWN STAMP

Although there is a huge range of rubber stamps available, it can be fun to make your own. Here are two simple ways to do so.

LINO-CUT STAMP
Carve a motif into an eraser using a lino-cutting tool.

1 Place the eraser on thin white paper. Draw around it with a soft pencil, and then draw your motif within the box. You need to draw the design to produce the print you want to achieve, so shade in black the areas that you want to print and leave blank the areas that you need to carve out.

2 Take the completed design and place it shaded side down on the eraser. Rub on the back of the paper to transfer the design, and then draw around the outline to make it stand out. Hold the eraser securely and, using the lino-cutting tool, carve around the edge of the pencil line that defines the motif. Hold the tool so the blade is flat side down (so that you can see the open 'V' shape) with the handle tucked into your palm.

3 Once the outline is complete, start carving out the background in a series of horizontal lines   you will find it easier to carve from the centre to the outside. Don't worry about carving it all away – a few fine lines will add interest.

4 Make a practise print onto scrap paper to see if you need to adjust your carving.

DIE CUT STAMP
You can use die-cut foam motifs to make a stamp. Remove the backing and place on a Rocker™ – these are a slightly curved form of mounting block that are used with self-adhesive foam. Pictured here, two separate stamps have been made that combine to make a butterfly motif.

tip As an eraser has two sides, you can carve one side for a trial run.

HEAT EMBOSSING

Heat embossing is a quicker and easier technique than may first appear. The motif is printed, sprinkled with embossing powder, and then heated to create a raised image. This then provides a framework for adding colour. While it is most often done over stamped images, there is no reason why you can't emboss stencilled or hand-drawn lines too.

HEAT EMBOSSING TOOLS

There are a few essential tools and materials that you will need for this technique.

tip If you use some powders on a regular basis, it is worth storing them in shallow containers with lids, with a spoon inside ready for use.

EMBOSSING POWDERS
These come in a variety of types that basically fall into the following categories: metallic and coloured (opaque); pearlescent (semi-transparent); glitter or sparkly (opaque, semi-transparent or clear); clear (transparent). Always check the label to find out which type the powder is so that you can choose the appropriate inkpad for stamping.

HEAT GUN AND HEAT-RESISTANT BOARD
A heat gun is used to melt the particles of the embossing powder together so that they form a plastic skin. There are several different models of heat gun on the market, so try to see them in action to select the right one for you. Always protect your work surface from the intense heat. A heat-resistant board is essential.

ANTI-STATIC PUFF
Before stamping, you should wipe the card with an anti-static puff to greatly reduce the risk of excess powder sticking to it. Not only does it combat static, but also it helps counteract any moisture, which some cards absorb more than others.

tip Never use a heat gun over a cutting mat as it will warp.

HOW TO HEAT EMBOSS

Practise your embossing technique first, and take the time to explore different ink and embossing powder combinations.

USING AN EMBOSSING INKPAD

1 Stamp your image on white card using a clear or tinted embossing inkpad – a tinted inkpad will make it easier for you to see where you have stamped the image.

2 Sprinkle the embossing powder carefully over the image. Apply just enough powder to cover the image. You may find it easier to sprinkle the powder with a spoon.

3 Gently shake off the excess powder onto a clean piece of paper and put aside. The wetness of the ink will hold the powder in place over the stamped image. Check for any areas that you may have missed. Brush any stray specks away with a fine paintbrush before heating.

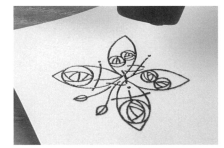

tip To save excess powder, fold the paper used to catch the excess powder in half first to create a funnel. Pour the powder back into the jar.

4 Hold the heat gun at least 2.5cm (1in) away from the surface and move it around from one area to the next as the powder melts. Work in good light so that you can see the image changing as the powder melts. Once the whole image has risen and turned shiny, stop heating. If you overheat the image, it will sink into the card and appear oily.

5 Once embossed, the image can be coloured using felt-tip pens, colouring pencils or paints. The raised outline makes it easier to keep the colouring medium within the outline of the image.

INK AND EMBOSSING POWDER COMBINATIONS

It can sometimes be useful to stamp an image using the same colour that will be used for embossing, especially if you miss any areas in the embossing process. Gold on gold works well, but try these other combinations for different effects.

For a stronger colour
- Copper embossing powder over brown ink.
- Black embossing powder over black ink.

For a softer colour
- Pearlescent blue embossing powder over black ink.
- Pearlescent gold embossing powder over gold ink.

USING EMBOSSING PENS

Embossing pens contain slow-drying ink to allow you time to colour in an image and emboss it. Any colour embossing powder can be used, although the clear ones will obviously let the colour of the pens show through. Available in four different tips – bullet, brush, and small and large chisel – these pens can also be used for freehand lettering and drawing. The pen colours are so bold that they are best combined with strong, graphic images.

1 Draw your design freehand onto your selected card.

2 Liberally apply embossing powder over and shake off the excess.

3 As you heat with a heat gun the image will become raised.

MULTI EMBOSSING

Embossing with a single powder is straightforward, but when you start to use more than one colour, the outcome is even more exciting. The application of the powder needs to be more precise and controlled for successful results.

1 Choose coloured embossing powders that will go together well and which complement your chosen card colour. Here amethyst, ruby and sapphire PearlLustre™ embossing powders have been chosen for use on a turquoise pearlescent card.

2 Sprinkle small quantities of the first embossing powder at random over the stamped image. Be sure to leave gaps for the other layers. Shake off the excess and heat.

3 Apply the second and third colours in the same way. You can apply the three colours in any order, but bear in mind that the last colour usually has the least coverage.

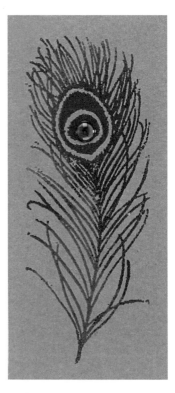

tip Put the excess embossing powder from applying the second and third colours in a separate container for a new colour.

DRY EMBOSSING

The term embossing is used to describe two particular techniques in crafting: one is the creation of a raised image on paper or card by applying pressure with an embossing tool, often working through a stencil; and the other is working on paper vellum with the embossing tool to change the colour of the paper for a decorative effect, and is often worked over a stamped image.

RELIEF EMBOSSING

Here, embossing refers to the technique of making a raised image on paper by applying pressure. The fibres of the paper are stretched to make a new shape, but the colour does not change as it does when embossing on vellum.

EMBOSSING TOOLS

There are a few key tools that you will need: the embossing tool and either embossing stencils or an embossing system, such as the Fiskars® ShapeBoss™.

Embossing tools: the size of the smooth metal ball attached to the handle varies from fine, through medium to large. The size of embossing tool required would depend on the size of the pattern on the stencil you are using.

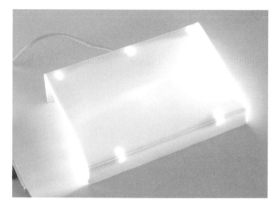

Light box: a light source is required when using stencils as the paper is placed over the stencil and without light behind it, it can be very difficult to see.

Stencils: metal stencils are available in a variety of patterns. Not all of the design on a stencil has to be embossed and this allows you to get more from your stencils by bringing together elements of several stencils.

The use of an embossing system means a light box is not necessary. They are very easy to use.

USING STENCILS AND A LIGHT BOX

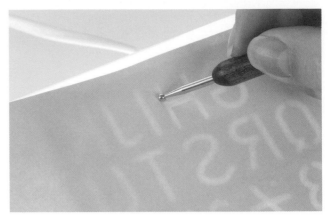

1 Place the stencil on the light box. If you are using letters or numbers, the stencil needs to be placed wrong side down so that they appear back to front as you work. Place the wrong side of your paper over the top of the stencil so that the raised image will appear the right way around on the right side. Press into the edges of the stencil with the medium ball embossing tool to outline the image.

2 Use the large ball embossing tool to emboss the inner areas. The weight of the paper or card you are using will influence how hard you need to press.

In these examples, the letter on the left did not have enough pressure applied; to rectify, line up the template with the design and go over it again. The middle letter is embossed with the correct amount of pressure, but too much pressure was applied to the letter on the right, causing the paper to tear.

USING AN EMBOSSING SYSTEM

With Fiskars® ShapeBoss™ stencil set, there are two identical plastic stencils, labelled top and bottom. These are secured in the tray with pegs. Lift up the stencil labelled 'top' and insert a sheet of paper in between the two stencil layers and then emboss just as you would if you were using a stencil over a light box.

For the Birthday Chef card the Creative Sampler set on the Fiskars® ShapeBoss™ was used to emboss an elongated 'S' shape five times, one above the other, moving the paper up and across slightly in the tool to create the appearance of steam, but not always embossing the whole shape. Using a soft-tip applicator, a blue blending chalk was rubbed on one side of the steam embossing to give it definition.

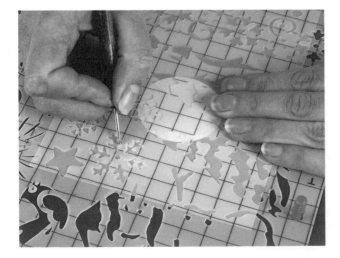

EMBOSSING ON VELLUM

Vellum is a translucent paper readily available in a variety of thicknesses, colours and patterns. Thicker vellum changes colour when pressure is applied to give a frosted finish. This technique is also known as parchment craft.

Always choose a thick, strong variety of vellum to reduce the risk of puncturing the surface and spoiling the paper.

USING A BALL EMBOSSING TOOL

1 The image to be embossed can either be stamped or drawn by hand. Rub the end of a fine ball embossing tool in the palm of your hand to pick up oil from your skin so that it will glide more easily over the surface of the vellum.

2 Always emboss vellum over a foam mat, working on the wrong side. Use the dry embossing tool to draw over an area several times to achieve a raised surface and frosted finish. Use an even pressure to avoid puncturing the vellum.

3 You can use a variety of patterns. For example, lines can emphasize the outline of the area being embossed, while dots, crosses and swirls can add decorative patterning.

You can outline the design with an embossing tool (as on the leaves) or use a ball embossing tool to fill in an area (as on the grapes); this detail is taken from the Vintage Celebration card (Life's Special Moments).

The harder you press, the darker the mark will appear; in this way you can choose to highlight areas of your design as seen on the Wedding Bouquet card (Life's Special Moments)..

On this detail from Polar Fun (The Cardmaker's Calendar) a fine ball embossing tool is used to make short, deep flicked marks for the bear's fur, with areas of lighter cross hatching in places.

PUNCHING

Decorative punching is a quick way to make basic, identical shapes from paper and card. They are easy-to-use, but with a little imagination they can have endless creative possibilities.

TYPES OF PUNCH

Punches are available in a wide variety of sizes and shapes. These are a good investment in order to make identical repeat images and can last a long time.

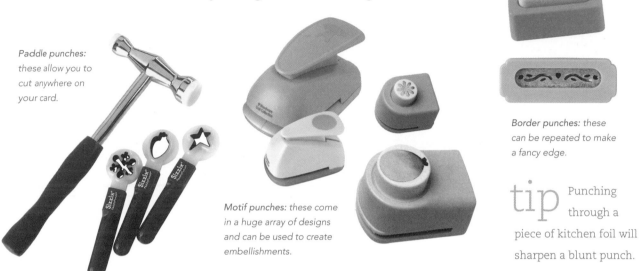

Paddle punches: these allow you to cut anywhere on your card.

Motif punches: these come in a huge array of designs and can be used to create embellishments.

Border punches: these can be repeated to make a fancy edge.

tip Punching through a piece of kitchen foil will sharpen a blunt punch.

HOW TO PUNCH

Work over a foam pad to protect your work surface and to prevent slipping. You may need to stand up when punching to apply more pressure to the punch. The shape that is punched out can be used as the main feature of a card or to embellish a design.

BASIC PUNCHING
Slide the paper into the punch. Apply firm downward pressure to the punch using your fingers or the palm of your hand. Don't discard the shape that is punched out of the paper: this negative can be retained and also used.

BASIC POSITIONING
By placing the punch upside down, with the cutter uppermost, you are able to position your paper accurately in the punch. Some punches have plastic covers on the bottom to catch punched pieces – remove this to see where you are placing the paper.

DIE-CUTTING

A die-cutting machine enables you to cut shapes from paper, foil or even fabric to embellish your cards quickly and professionally, and it makes light work of repeat shapes, especially when you are making cards in bulk, as at Christmas. There are hundreds of designs to choose from.

DIE-CUTTING TOOLS

A large die-cutting tool, such as the one shown here, is a big investment for a crafter, although there are many other types available that are smaller, more portable and less expensive. The die-cut templates must be purchased separately, but if you have a crafting friend with a compatible machine, you could swap templates to give you a wider range of shapes to use.

tip Pre-cut die-cut shapes can also be purchased by theme.

Electronic cutting machines such as the lightweight Cricut® are also available. The Cricut® is a stand-alone machine that does not require a computer. Simply plug into a power source, choose your cartridge (the machine comes with a starter [George] cartridge), and at the touch of a button beautiful designs can be cut tailored to your requirements.

USING A HAND-OPERATED DIE-CUT MACHINE

1 Place the base plastic sheet and die-cut in the die-cutting tool. Position a piece of patterned paper, printed side up, over the die-cut. Add the top plastic sheet. Turn the handle to die-cut the shape.

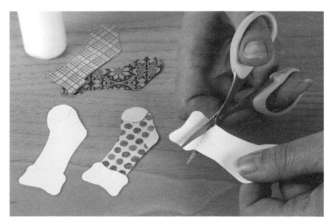

2 Some die cuts will have perforations, allowing the shape to be cut several times on several different pieces of paper and card, and then the elements can be cut and combined together for creative results. The Quick-to-Make Stocking card is an example of this. Stockings were die-cut from both patterned and white card. Then the perforations at the top, toe and heel of the white card stockings were cut with a small pair of scissors, and attached to the patterned paper stockings.

QUILLING

Paper quilling (or paper filigree) is the craft of coiling thin strips of paper. These coils are glued and then pinched into different shapes. The resulting shapes make wonderful decorations for cards. To start quilling, a quilling tool is recommended, but it is possible to make coils just by using your fingers.

QUILLER'S TOOLS AND MATERIALS

Although it is possible to cut paper strips yourself and coil them using just your fingers, if you are going to use quilling for your card decorations often, it will make sense to invest in some purpose made tools.

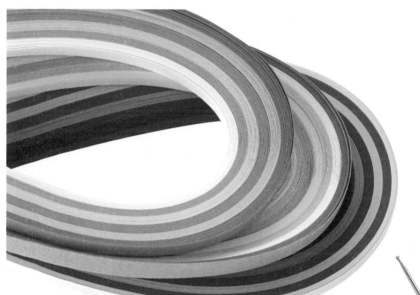

QUILLING PAPER STRIPS

Pre-cut strips are available in many standard widths and colours. Those popularly used are:

1.5 or 2mm (¹⁄16in) The minimum width that is available.

3mm (¹⁄8in) The most common width and ideal for beginners.

5mm (³⁄16in) Good for freestanding 3D quilling work.

1cm (³⁄8in) The most common width for use with a fringing tool.

1.5cm (⁵⁄8in) Some suppliers offer this width for making frilly flowers with the adjustable 90 degree-angled fringing tools.

QUILLING TOOLS

These come in all shapes and sizes, but all consist of a two-pronged slot through which a paper strip is threaded. It is important to find the tool that suits you. Some people prefer long handles, while others favour shorter ones that fit into the palm of the hand. When choosing, check the size of the gap at the curling end. A large gap means a large hole in the centre of the coil, which is most noticeable when making tight closed coils. Two of the quilling tools shown opposite comprise a sewing needle with one end snipped off embedded into a wooden handle. These have a gap just wide enough to slot the paper through to create a very small central hole in a tight coil. The needle tool is useful for rolling paper around to leave a hole in the centre.

Quilling tools.

Needle tool.

Self-locking fine-tipped tweezers.

Small, fine-pointed scissors.

FRINGING TOOL

A fringing tool enables you to fringe narrow paper strips with speed and precision. Various types are available depending on the size of paper strip you are working with, and whether you want to cut at a 90 degree or 45 degree angle. Place a 1cm (³⁄₈in) wide strip of paper in the tool. Move the handle up and down – the paper is sliced width ways but not all the way across leaving a narrow margin to keep the strips of paper in one piece. At the same time, the paper strip is pulled along so that it is automatically fed through the slicer.

COILING

The technique of coiling is fundamental to quilling.

1 Insert a strip of paper into the slot of the quilling tool 2mm (¹⁄₁₆in) from the end of the paper strip. Here, a 3mm (¹⁄₈in) wide paper strip is used.

2 Turn the quilling tool to catch the end of the paper strip.

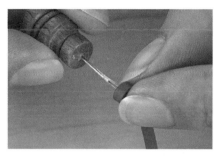

3 Continue to turn the tool. Guide the coil with your fingers and keep a light tension on the paper with your spare hand.

4 Continue turning to the end of the strip of paper, then carefully remove the tool by sliding the paper off the prongs, holding the coil in place.

5 Add a dot of glue to the end of the paper strip with a cocktail stick (toothpick) or fine-tip applicator and adhere to the coil to create a tight closed coil.

6 Alternatively, release the coil a little and then glue the end of the strip to the coil to create a shape with thick edges – a loose closed coil. If you release the coil further, it becomes larger in size.

7 Alternatively, use a quilling board to achieve a specific size of coil.

CREATING SHAPES

The basic coiling technique can be built upon to create shapes from the closed coils. The best effects are achieved using loose closed coils, where the end of the paper has been glued to the coil, but the coil has been allowed to unwind a little so that it becomes loose while remaining closed. The basic coil can then be pinched between the thumb and index finger at one or more points to form a variety of shapes as shown below.

Teardrop Pinch at one point.

Crescent Pinch at two opposing points, then pull the pinched points round and inwards to bend.

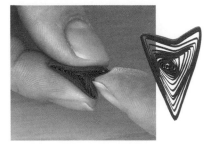

Heart Hold the coil in one hand and pinch at one point while simultaneously pushing inwards with a fingernail at the opposing point.

Triangle Pinch at three equally-spaced points.

Square Pinch at two opposing points and at another equally spaced two points; push two opposing points in opposite directions to form a square.

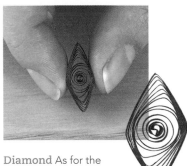

Diamond As for the square, but stood on one point.

QUILLED EMBELLISHMENTS

Some of the cards featured in this book require particular shapes and embellishments to be made.

TO MAKE OPEN QUILLED HEARTS
This shape is required for the Wedding Cake Congratulations (Life's Special Moments).

1 For a large heart, wrap a 20cm (8in) length of 3mm (1/8in) wide paper around a wooden spoon handle or dowel 1.5cm (5/8in) in diameter. Glue the end in place and remove.

2 Pinch at one point while pushing the opposing point inwards. Make two smaller hearts from 10cm (4in) lengths wrapped around a wooden spoon or dowel with a 1cm (3/8in) diameter.

3 Place a small dot of glue in the top centre crease and a little on the underside of the crease (not the copper-edged side). Using tweezers, pinch the inner point and hold for a few seconds.

TO MAKE A FRINGED AND COILED FLOWER
This decoration is used on the Beautiful Blooms card (Birthdays).

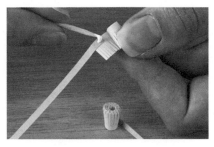

1 Fringe a 15cm (6in) length of 1cm (³⁄8in) wide cream paper strip. Using a cocktail stick (toothpick), glue a 4cm (1½in) length of 3mm (1⁄8in) yellow paper strip to the margin at one end of the fringed cream strip. Glue a 12cm (4¾in) length of 3mm (1⁄8in) light green paper strip to the margin on the other end of the fringed cream strip. Leave the glue to dry. Place the yellow paper strip in the quilling tool and coil tightly until you reach the green strip.

2 Carefully remove the quilling tool. Using a cocktail stick (toothpick), apply a dab of glue to the beginning of the green strip. Press this onto the rest of the coiled paper.

3 When the glue has dried, open out the cream fringed part to reveal the yellow centre of the flower.

tip When posting a quilled card, place two layers of bubble wrap in the envelope to protect it from being crushed.

TO MAKE A DAFFODIL TRUMPET
This shape is required for the St David's Day card (The Cardmaker's Calendar).

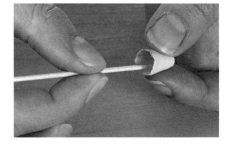

1 Cut along the edge of a strip of 10mm (³⁄8in) wide yellow paper using fancy-edged scissors. Glue a 20cm (8in) length of the same yellow paper to a 40cm (15¾ in) length end to end, then glue a 10cm (4in) length of the fancy-edged strip to the end of this. For stamens, cut four strips of the orange paper about 1mm x 1.5cm (1⁄16 x 5⁄8in) and glue to the plain end.

2 Starting at the plain end, make a tight coil for a length of about 20cm (8in), then angle the paper away from the tool, making sure that it overlaps, to form a cone shape. This becomes quite a challenge towards the end, so coil slowly and carefully. Glue the end in place.

3 Move the orange stamens to one side and use a cocktail stick (toothpick) to apply glue inside the trumpet around the side. Leave to dry.

TO MAKE A CARROT BUNCH

Carrot embellishments are required for Sweet Treat (The Cardmaker's Calendar) and His Vegetable Patch (Birthdays).

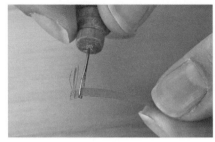

1 For the carrot roots, cut a 1.3cm (½in) length of the 3mm (⅛ in) wide orange paper into four very narrow strands, but leave them joined at the end. Glue to the end of a 20cm (8in) length of orange paper for the carrot itself.

2 Position the quilling tool to the left of the strands, with the strands hanging downwards, and begin to turn the tool to coil the paper tightly for a few turns.

3 Continue turning the quilling tool, but as you do so, angle the paper away from the tool, so that as you coil it creates a cone shape. When coiling, make sure that the paper overlaps, but vary the overlaps to make the cone uneven. Secure the end of the paper with glue. Apply a generous coating of glue inside the cone with a cocktail stick (toothpick) and leave to dry.

TO MAKE OPEN 'S' COILS

4 For the leaves, fold a length of 1cm (⅜in) green paper in half along its length and use a 45 degree fringing tool to fringe. Cut the fringed paper into 5cm (2in) lengths. Keeping the paper folded in half, trim the fringes for a length of 1.5cm (⅝in) from one end, leaving the uncut margin as a stalk. Make random cuts into the fringing before unfolding and opening

5 Round the tip of the leaf. You will need three or four leaves per carrot. Glue the leaf stalks to the end of a 10cm (4in) length of orange paper and start coiling from the end with the leaves. Make a tight coil. Apply a generous amount of glue inside the top of the carrot cone, then insert the tight coil.

Make open 'S' coils (Wedding Cake Congratulations card) with 4cm (1½in) lengths of 3mm (⅛in) paper by coiling into the centre from one end inwards, then coiling from the other end outwards. Some scrolls are made with the copper edge in the tool up and some copper-edge down. When positioning the scrolls on the card, insert the quilling tool back into the centre of each scroll to help position it and re-coil if necessary.

tip To make handles for the Shear Delight card make a narrow cone shape with a smaller overlap using a 9cm (3½in) length of cream paper, but handle delicately as it will be quite fragile.

PEEL-OFF STICKERS

There is an almost endless range of ready-to-use designs and motifs, available in a variety of different forms, such as outline, solid, embossed, 3D and resin. Also available are different styles of lettering, numbers and borders. They are a fun way to make a card in minutes or to add those all important finishing touches.

Peel-off stickers can be bought in themed sheets. There are thousands to choose from, from pretty flowers and decorative motifs to practical eyelets and text messages.

BASIC TECHNIQUES

Large solid stickers are easy to use, but outline peel-offs and small stickers will need a little more care.

Remove and transfer small peel-off stickers with a craft knife.

Never hold an outline peel-off with two hands as this will stretch it out of shape.

tip Flatter than peel-off stickers, rub-on transfers can be transferred to paper or card by rubbing with the back of a teaspoon.

MAKING THE MOST OF PEEL-OFF STICKERS

Here are a few tricks to get even more from your peel-off stickers.

To make into an embellishment, stick the outline peel-offs onto coloured vellum or card, leaving enough room to cut around each one. Use small fine-tipped scissors or snips and go right up to the edge of the sticker, but be careful not to cut the edge. To fix to the card, use an adhesive foam pad on the back.

Outline peel-off stickers can also be used to add a stencilled background to a plain base card. Stick the peel-off anywhere on the card. Dip a piece of sponge into an inkpad and use to apply ink over and around the sticker. Carefully remove the sticker; re-position and repeat until the whole background is covered.

Stickers can be used imaginatively. Smiley face stickers have been used on the Flip-Up Phone Card (Birthdays) to make a mobile (cell) phone keypad.

tip Make your own stickers using a Xyron™ machine with an adhesive cartridge to apply glue to the reverse of punched or cut out shapes.

IRIS FOLDING

Iris folding is a paper folding technique involving laying strips of patterned paper across a shaped aperture, working from the outside inwards, until they eventually meet, forming a spiral. The spiral resembles the iris of an eye or a camera, and this is how the technique got its name. Depending on the papers used, an almost kaleidoscopic, psychedelic effect can be produced.

TOOLS AND MATERIALS

No specialist tools are required apart from a folding template, and, once you have the experience, you can even design these yourself. A pair of small, fine-pointed pair of scissors is needed for trimming the paper strips and clear adhesive tape to attach the strips, and although specific papers for iris folding are available, any patterned, lightweight papers can be used. It is essential, however, that lightweight papers are used or the many layers of folded papers become too bulky.

tip Make your own iris folding paper by stamping patterns on lightweight coloured paper, then cut into strips.

THE BASIC TECHNIQUE

Choose papers that complement each other. In the example below, three colours are used for the basic triangle shape, but if using a square or circle aperture, four or five strips of paper may work better.

1 Place the iris folding template underneath a piece of card that has an aperture cut in it the same shape and size as the template. Cut and fold in half lengthways strips of paper.

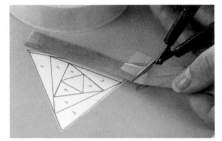

2 Following the numbered sequence, place the strips of paper in turn, taking care to line up with the lines on the template and making sure that the folds are facing inwards for a crisp, clean effect. Secure with small pieces of clear tape and trim the excess paper so the remaining paper overlaps the edge of the aperture.

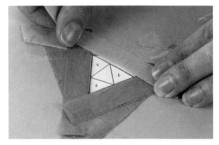

3 Continue to build up the strips in this way until they have all been used up.

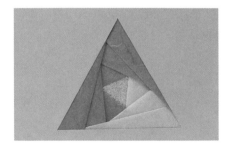

4 Tape a small piece of holographic paper over the hole left in the centre. Turn over to admire the finished design.

tip Iris folding originated in the Netherlands, where the colourful insides of envelopes were recycled for this papercraft.

TEA BAG FOLDING

Also known as kaleidoscope folding, tea bag folding creates amazing patterns from tiny squares of paper. There are lots of specialist papers available for this technique, but you can create your own, as long as each square has an identical pattern and each square is cut in exactly the same place.

FOLDING THE BASIC UNIT

Learn how to fold the basic unit, and then explore how you can put together the origami-based shapes to create even more patterns. When using patterned paper begin folding with the same section of pattern facing you.

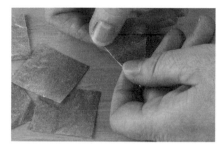

1 Fold one piece of 5cm (2in) square paper from corner to corner with the right side up. Open, then fold it from corner to corner using the opposite corners. Open it out.

2 Fold the paper in half horizontally. Open it out again. You have now made three mountain folds on the paper.

3 Turn the paper over and fold it in half lengthways, where there is no fold, wrong sides out. This creates a valley fold on the right side.

4 Open out the paper again and turn it to the right side. Push the valley fold in and flatten the paper to form a triangle.

5 Fold the top corners in to the centre to make a point.

6 To make a rosette, make four units. Cut a 2.5cm (1in) circle of scrap card and stick the folded shapes on top.

tip Rub the folded edges with a bone folder for a crisp finish.

To keep the points of your folded papers flat, use a tiny amount of glue underneath the folds.

3D DECOUPAGE

From the French word 'découpager', meaning to cut out, découpage is the craft of cutting out pre-printed pictures; 3D découpage involves layering those pictures, separated by silicone gel, to give dimension to the image. The Batsman's Birthday card has been made using this technique. You can buy découpage papers, which have repeated identical images, to appeal to all sorts of interests

THE BASIC TECHNIQUE

As you need to use a lot of glue for this technique, it is sensible to protect your work surface with a sheet of scrap paper.

1 Cut out four cricket pictures and put one aside for Step 3. Place a small amount of PVA (white) glue on the centre of the wrong side of a cricket picture, then use a small piece of clean scrap card to pull the glue from the centre outwards and over the edges, going over onto the scrap paper. Stick onto white card.

2 Repeat with the other two images and leave to dry (the paper may wrinkle a little but you can place them under a pile of books to flatten them). Using a small pair of scissors, cut out two cricketers, one set of stumps and three ball shapes. You may find it easier to roughly cut around each shape first and then cut each piece out neatly.

3 Hold the first cut-out cricketer with tweezers with a locking device, which saves you from continuously having to apply pressure, and apply dots of silicone gel to the wrong side – be sure to work in a well-ventilated room to avoid inhaling any fumes. Place the cut out directly over the cricketer in the complete picture set aside. Repeat with the cut-out stumps and ball, placing each directly over its counterpart.

4 Mount a second cut-out cricketer layer using the same technique. You don't need to wait until the first layer of gel is dry, but you may find it easier and it dries within a few hours. Mount the two remaining cut-out cricket balls.

5 When you are ready to fix the découpage panel to your decorated base card, hold it with tweezers in an old cardboard box, in a well-ventilated space (preferably outdoors), and apply spray glue evenly to the wrong side.

With 3D découpage the image literally leaps out from the card and so it is ideal for action images such as this.

techniques ● 3D DECOUPAGE

METAL AND WIRE

Available as sheet, ready-made shapes or fine leaf, metal can be used to decorate cards in a variety of ways, including heat and dry embossing. Wire is a flexible and versatile material that can be formed into coils and motifs. Wire cutters or pliers can be useful for cutting and bending, but many thinner metals and wires can just as easily be cut with scissors.

CREATIVE OPTIONS

Just a few of the creative options for metal and wire are illustrated below.

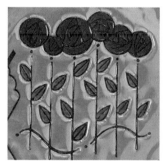

Embellishments attached to a wire coil can make for an action-packed card design. This monkey face is made by simply layering five circles, but a sticker could be used.

When drawing a continuous line into a foil surface, the metal can sometimes buckle up as it is pushed along; by using a broken line, bumps and notches can be avoided.

Pure copper sheeting is pliable and easy to work with. It is thin enough to punch shapes from yet holds an embossed pattern well. If heated, it will change colour most attractively, but purchase carefully as coated copper-coloured metal sheets will not give the desired effect.

tip *If you don't have wire cutters, use scissors for thinner metals and wire; cut near to the base of the scissors.*

MAKING A WIRE COIL

For a dynamic card, a wire coil can have card motifs attached. Wrap a relatively sturdy but pliable wire around a tube-shaped item. Here a 24-gauge wire has been formed around a pencil, but try wrapping other weights of wire around other tube-shaped items to make springs in other diameters – knitting needles, for example, are ideal for making springs in a variety of sizes.

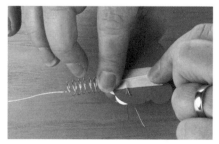

1 Cut three 30cm (12in) lengths of silver wire using wire cutters or snips. Leaving a straight section 2–3cm (1in) long at the beginning, start to wind the first piece of wire around a pencil.

2 Complete the spiral, leaving another 2–3cm (1in) straight section at the other end. Use a pair of round-nosed pliers to bend the wire at right angles at each end, flat to the pencil. Make sure that the straight sections are in line.

3 Attach one straight end of wire to the back of the card decoration using masking tape, ensuring that the spiral starts just at the bottom of the motif.

MAKING ENVELOPES

As well as providing extra protection during transit in the mail, bespoke presentation and packaging can complement and enhance the look of your handmade cards. Envelopes can be tailored to fit exactly and customized and coordinated to match the card inside, while the box envelope is ideal for your 3D designs, including those that have quilled or wire embellishments.

MAKING A BASIC ENVELOPE

It is easy to make an envelope to fit the exact size of your card. Start by making a template of your card.

1 First make a template of your card. Measure the card front and draw onto scrap paper adding 3mm (⅛in) to each edge. At the top edge, draw the flap half the depth of the front. At the bottom edge, draw the envelope back taking 2cm (¾in) off the depth. Draw a tab at each side of the front 2.5cm (1in) wide and draw a curve at each corner.

2 Cut out and use the template to draw the envelope onto the wrong side of your chosen paper or thin card. Cut out, score and fold along the lines. Fold the side tabs in.

3 Apply double-sided tape along the side edges of the back, peel off the backing and stick over the side tabs. Insert your finished card and tuck the flap inside the envelope.

EASY SQUARE ENVELOPE

This easy-to-make envelope can be adapted to fit any size of square card, although the instructions provided are for a 12.5cm (5in) card. Choose four different colours to coordinate with colours/patterns used on the card design. These are used in a series of flaps, which interleave to encase the card, tied with sheer red ribbon.

1 Cut a 12.5cm (5in) square of card from each of the four different colours. Score and fold in half. Round off two corners on one side with a corner rounder. Open out one square and lay face down. Apply four lengths of double-sided adhesive tape around one quarter on the unrounded side.

2 Remove the tape backing and place the corner on top of a corner of another square, tucking the edge into the fold. Repeat with the other squares, then stick the last corners together. Glue the ribbon to the envelope back, insert the card and tie in a bow around the interleaved flaps.

USING A PLASTIC ENVELOPE TEMPLATE

The quickest and easiest way to make an envelope is to use a plastic envelope template. Some of these offer three different sizes on a single template to choose from to match your card. For the outer envelope, use a strong paper or lightweight card that is easy to fold, in a colour to coordinate with your design. For the lining, you can use a patterned paper to complement your card's theme.

tip Instead of making a separate liner, use a plain paper for the envelope, then print on the inside with a rubber stamp, to create a pattern before gluing the envelope sides in place.

1 Place the clear plastic envelope template on your chosen paper. (If it is printed paper with a busy design, use the plain side.) Draw around the template onto the paper. Here, a liner for the envelope was made by cutting out a smaller envelope from printed paper.

2 Place the liner inside the larger envelope and use a glue stick to glue in place. Fold the two outer flaps inwards. Fold the lower flap upwards. Apply glue to the two folded flaps, and then press the lower flap down onto the two folded flaps.

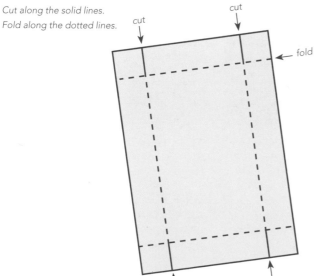

MAKING A BOX ENVELOPE

If sending 3D cards by post you will need to make a box envelope to accommodate its depth. This can be made exactly to fit in a few simple steps.

1 Measure the size of the finished greetings card and add 2.5cm (1in) to the height and width to determine the size of the card required for the base and the lid. Cut two pieces the same size. You could use a white or plain coloured card for the base, with a patterned card for the lid.

2 Take the lid piece and with a ruler and embossing tool or bone folder score a line 1cm (3/8in) in from the edge and parallel to each of the four sides.

3 With scissors carefully snip on the two long edges, only up to where the fold lines intersect, and then fold along the scored lines on all four sides.

4 Secure the folded flaps with double-sided tape or glue to complete the lid.

5 Take the base piece and carefully trim 3mm (1/8in) from the top and left-hand side only. Then follow the instructions for making the lid to make the base in the same way. Because the base is slightly smaller, the lid should fit comfortably over the top.

Cut along the solid lines.
Fold along the dotted lines.

cut
cut
fold
cut
cut
cut

TEMPLATES ACTUAL SIZE

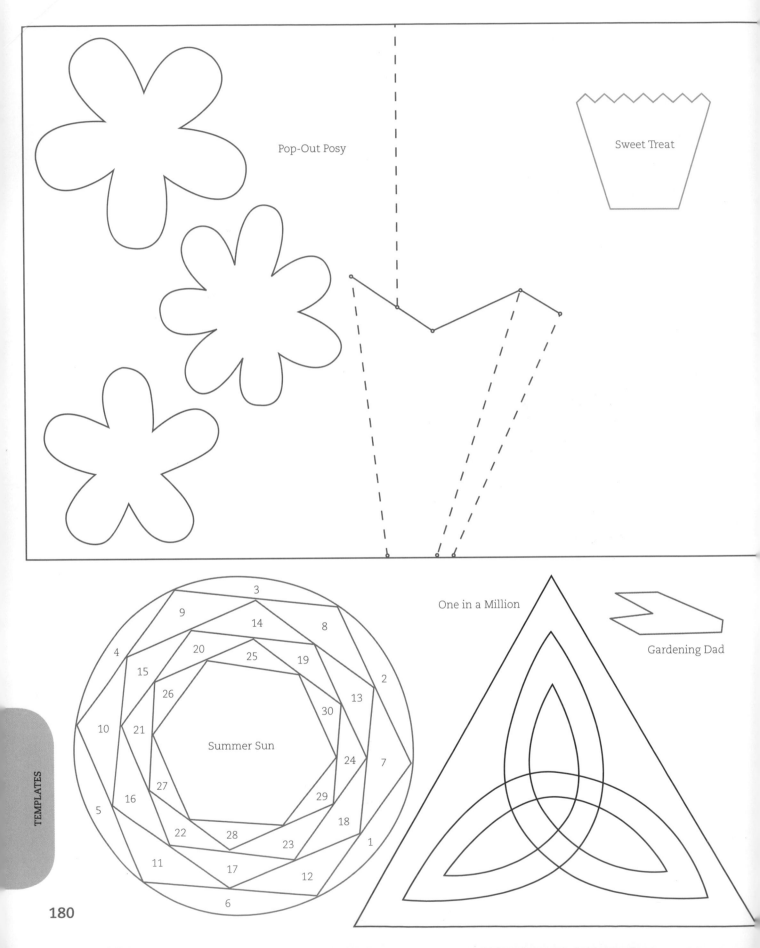

Pop-Out Posy

Sweet Treat

One in a Million

Gardening Dad

Summer Sun

3 9 14 8 20 25 19 4 15 26 2 10 21 13 30 16 27 24 7 5 22 28 29 18 11 17 23 1 6 12

TEMPLATES

Independence Day

Sweet Folding Chicks

Invitation to
Thanksgiving

sleeve

glass

bottle

label

turkey body

turkey leg

plate

181

haunted house

ghost

House Ghost

Action-Packed Birthday

cut

cut

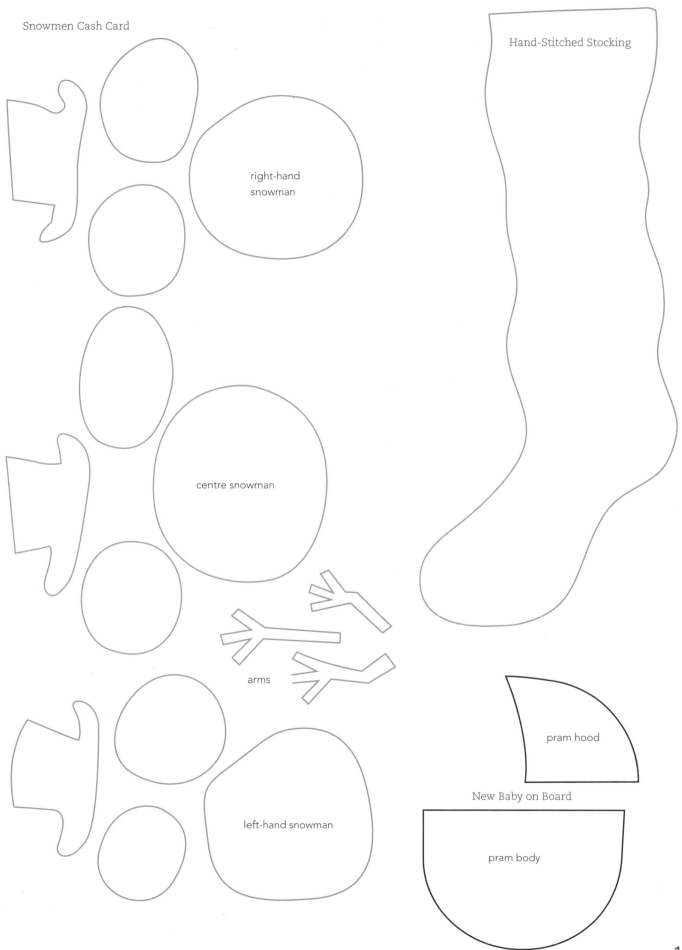

Snowmen Cash Card

right-hand
snowman

centre snowman

arms

left-hand snowman

Hand-Stitched Stocking

pram hood

New Baby on Board

pram body

Santa's Special Delivery

By Candlelight

Rudolph the Reindeer

Crowning Glory

The Happy Couple

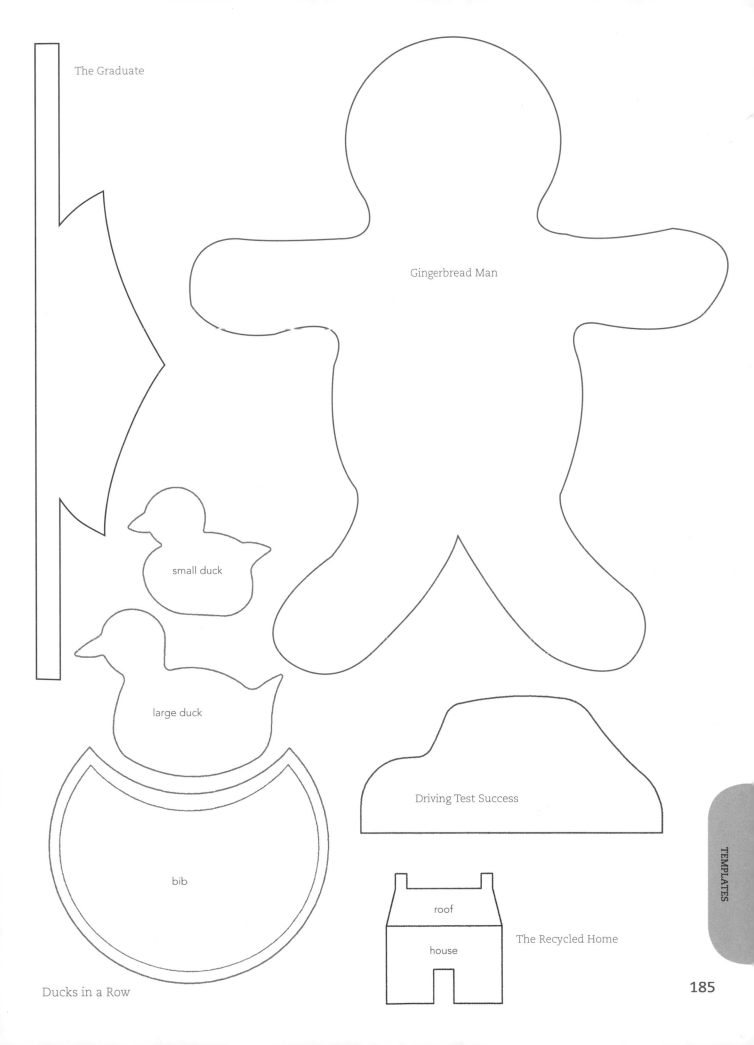

The Graduate

Gingerbread Man

small duck

large duck

bib

Driving Test Success

roof

house

The Recycled Home

Ducks in a Row

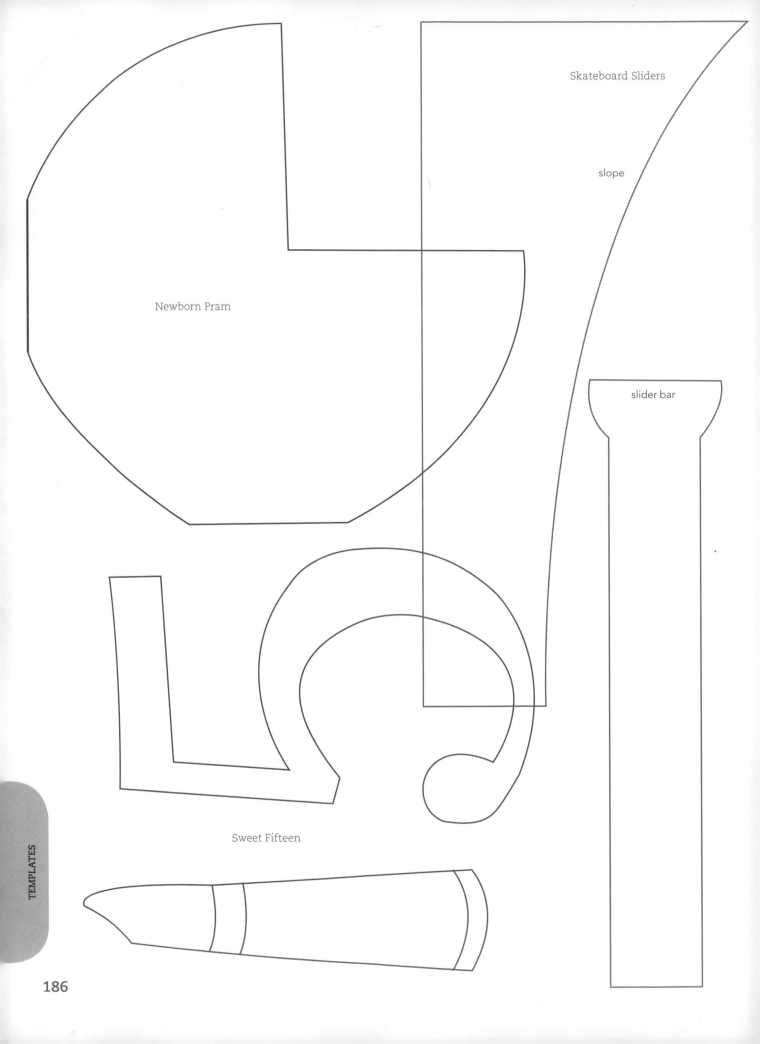

Skateboard Sliders

slope

Newborn Pram

slider bar

Sweet Fifteen

TEMPLATES

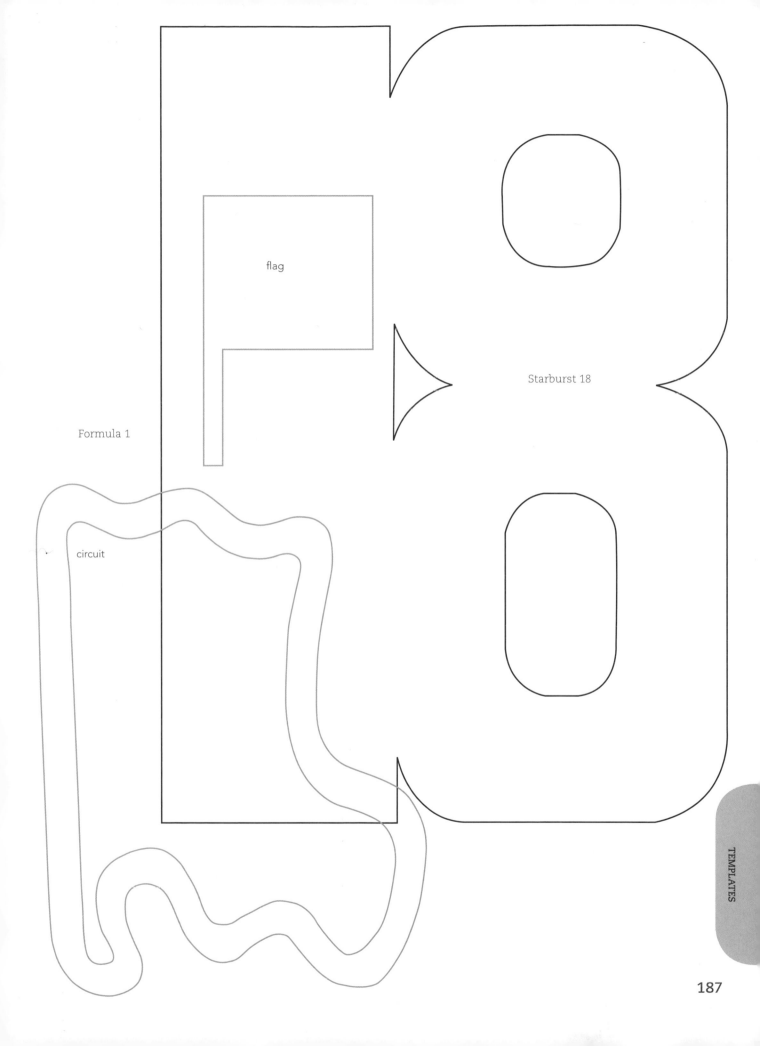

flag

Starburst 18

Formula 1

circuit

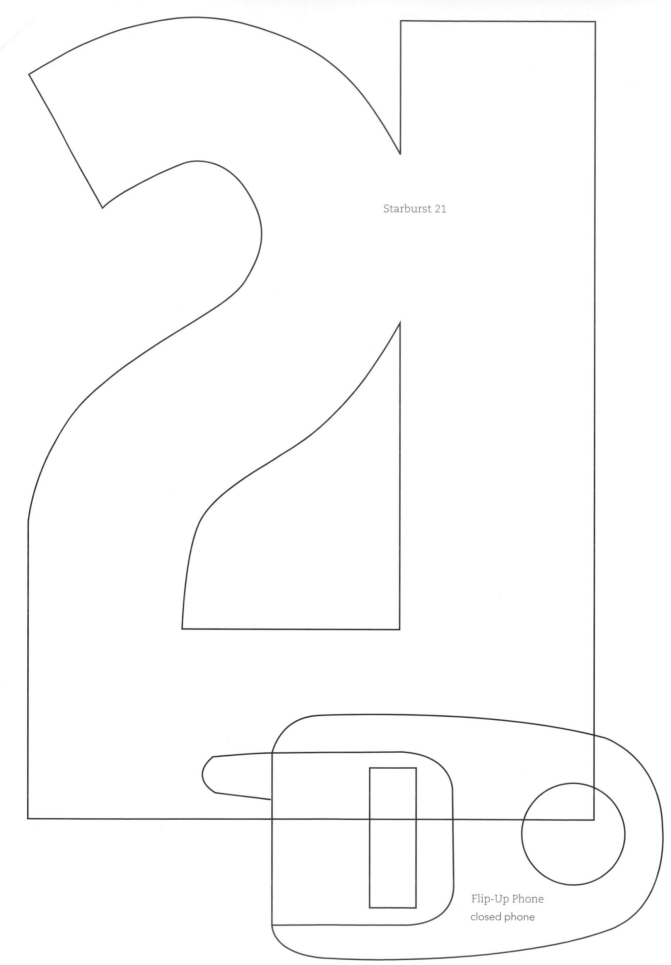

Starburst 21

Flip-Up Phone
closed phone

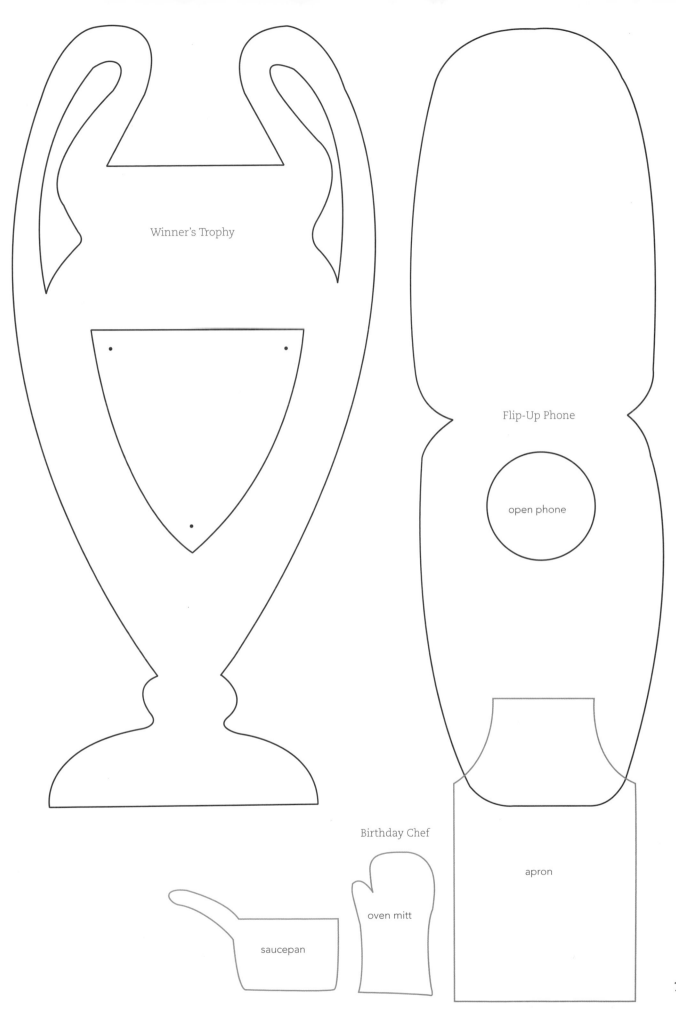

Winner's Trophy

Flip-Up Phone

open phone

Birthday Chef

saucepan

oven mitt

apron

The Card Designers

The cards in this book are the creations of a number of talented papercraft artists.

Corinne Bradd is a regular contributor and demonstrator for specialist craft magazines, including *Crafts Beautiful* who can regularly be seen on YouTube's 'Crafts Channel'. She has contributed to several cardmaking books and is the author of *Christmas Papercrafts*.

Marion Elliot is an artist and designer working in a variety of media, especially paper. A one-time designer for Hallmark, she is the author of several papercraft books including *Paper Sculpt Sensation* and *Cards for Tots to Teens*.

Julie Hickey is a successful cardmaker, papercrafts tutor and author. She is a product designer for Craftwork Cards and has appeared on Create and Craft TV. She has written several books including *Flower Power Papercrafts*, *Quick & Clever Handmade Cards* and *Quick & Clever Instant Cards*.

Elizabeth Moad runs workshops and contributes designs to several papercraft magazines. She has written several books including *Thrilling Quilling, Cards for Lads and Dads*, *The Papercrafter's Bible* and *Quick & Clever Christmas Cards*. For more information, see www.elizabethmoad.com.

Sue Nicholson has a passion for innovative card making and has run workshops, contributed to magazines and demonstrated at craft outlets as well as writing two successful books, *Surprisingly Simple Novelty Cards* and *Simply Sensational Scrapbook Cards*. For more information, see www.suenicholson.com.

Francoise Read was an arts and crafts secondary school teacher before turning her creative talents to designing stamps, peel-offs and other papercraft materials for companies including Woodware. She has written several books including *The Rubber Stamper's Bible* and *100 Great Ways to Use Rubber Stamps*.

Joanne Sanderson is both a talented cross stitch and papercraft designer. Her designs have featured regularly in magazines including *Card Making and PaperCraft* and she has demonstrated on dvds produced by Create and Craft TV. She has written several books including *3D Rubber Stamping*. For more information, see www.joannesanderson.com.

Shirley Toogood has worked as the technical editor for *Papercraft Inspirations* and many other craft magazines. Her passion for papercrafts resulted in her writing *100 Great Ways to Make Cards*.

Dorothy Wood has been writing craft books for over 20 years including some of the most successful beading books ever written. Her papercraft titles include the dynamic *Paper Pop Up*. For more information, see www.dorothywood.co.uk.

SUPPLIERS

The papercraft world changes fast and new products are coming out all the time, and just as quickly others are discontinued; specific details of the products used by the designers are not given therefore. It is hoped that the designers' product choices will inspire you to find similar papers, stamps, punches and embellishments from your favourite papercraft suppliers, but it is hoped, too, that you will be encouraged to substitute their selections for others more suited to your own individual tastes. Have fun exploring and below are some details of suppliers to get you started.

UK

Craft Hobbies and Haberdashery
www.craftyhobbiesuk.com

Crafts U Love
www.craftsulove.co.uk
01293 863576

Craftwork Cards
www.craftworkcards.co.uk
0113 2765713

Crafty Individuals
www.craftyindividuals.co.uk
01642 789955

Elusive Images
www.elusiveimages.com
01833 694914

Horseshoe Crafts
www.horseshoecrafts.co.uk
01691 690113

MIC
www.miccraft.net
01707 269999

Rubbadubbadoo
www.rubbadubbadoo.co.uk
01308 420802

The Scrapbook Shop
www.scrapbookshop.co.uk
0191 3757515

The Stamp Man
www.thestampman.co.uk
01756 797048

WhichCraft
www.whichcraft.co.uk
01302 810608

USA

Art Institute Glitter
www.artglitter.com
928-639-0805

Bazzill Paper
www.bazzillbasics.com

Clearsnap Inc
www.clearsnap.com
360-293-6634

Doodlebug Design Inc
www.doodlebug.ws
801-966-9952

EK Success
www.eksuccess.com
800-524-1349

Ellison
www.ellison.com/corp
949-598-8822

Fancy Pants
www.fancypantsdesigns.com

Making Memories
www.makingmemories.com

My Sentiments Exactly
www.sentiments.com
719-260-6001

Penny Black Rubber Stamps Inc
www.pennyblackinc.com
510-849-1883

Quickutz
www.quickutz.com
801-764-200

Stampin Up
www.stampinup.com

Stampendous Inc
www.stampendous.com
714-688-0288